Three-Dimensional Foremanship

THREE-DIMENSIONAL FOREMANSHIP

Frank A. Busse

American Management Association, Inc.

To Peg, my wife,
the greatest practitioner of good foremanship
for our children and me

PREFACE

THIS IS A BOOK of philosophy and techniques for the American foreman—the manager, supervisor, and instructor of his men. Each chapter of the book develops the basic foreman–employee relationship in business establishments and attempts to resolve the problems encountered by the foreman in his day-to-day work.

America can be justifiably proud of its industrial strength and its present know-how, capacity, and power. At the apex of the industrial triangle are some of the largest manufacturing and business enterprises in the world. At the base are the thousands of small businesses that make up the solid foundation of the American free-enterprise economy.

The large corporations have long since established development programs for all management levels, both line and staff. However, many of the small industrial and commercial units at the base of the triangle, especially those that are relatively new, have not progressed to this point and lack a centralized personnel function to assist the line foreman. In many cases this foreman is a young person, bright and technically well equipped, but with little knowledge of the human relations aspects of his job. He is often beset with "people" problems that take well over 50 percent of his time. Top management may not be aware of his need or, even if it is, may feel that the company is too small to be able to afford formal programs headed by a director of supervisory development.

This book has been written for these foremen who are searching for solutions to their problems and who want to learn how to do their jobs better.

Much of the book is based on personal experience in management, beginning as a factory foreman many years ago when there was no available assistance. However, most of the philosophies and techniques set forth here are not new and have been tried and found to work successfully over the years.

Although the term "foreman" has been used almost exclusively throughout the book, the information in it is not necessarily limited to those people who hold the title "foreman." It should be equally helpful to anyone, regardless of title, who directs the efforts of one or more people. Nor should the inference be drawn that this information is "for men only." It pertains equally to the many women in leadership positions, whether they have the title "forelady," "supervisor," or "office manager."

Rarely is a book completed solely by one person, and this is not one of those rare cases. It would not be possible to acknowledge by name all those who have contributed ideas, but many friends and associates have been an inspiration through their encouragement and criticism over the years. Specifically, the author acknowledges the constant guidance and help of Phil Carroll and the late Don F. Copell. Profound thanks go to Benjamin Werne, labor attorney, for his help with the chapters on labor unions and union contracts. And without the skilled help of Betty Cliffe, secretary, who laboriously translated a longhand scrawl into a legible page, the book could never have been completed.

FRANK A. BUSSE

CONTENTS

Three-Dimensional Foremanship

1

THE FOREMAN AND HIS JOB

PRIMITIVE PEOPLE, unschooled and quite unskilled, have always made things. People worked together in groups, with the tasks assigned according to their various skills by a chief selected from among the group. Each man had to do his share, and the chief made sure that he did it. There undoubtedly were differences among individual members of the group that the chief had to settle. True, the chief did not have cost problems, labor problems, and other modern problems to contend with, but he did have to be reasonably well liked and respected or the group would banish him and select another chief.

This method of work (groups under a chief or head man) was used for centuries without much change or refinement. There was no need for any. However, in the Middle Ages, craft guilds or organized groups made their appearance. (Guild halls more than 500 years old may still be seen in England.) The artisans of these craft guilds (actually the forerunners of unions) selected one of their group to "go to the fore" to represent the group with their masters and others. He thus became known as a "foreman." Today the foreman does not have the same function that he had in medieval days, although he does represent his employees to management. In fact, the word "foreman" does not have the same meaning in all plants and does not always carry with it the same responsibilities. There is a general understanding, however, that the term refers to any person with leadership responsibilities that place him in a position to direct the efforts of other people and to have responsible contact with the workforce on the one hand and with management on the other.

Many titles are applied to this important line function—"supervisor," "foreman," "leadman," "keyman," and others. Really, any person who is responsible for the work of one or more people is a supervisor (from the Latin *super* meaning "over" and *videre* meaning "to see"). Throughout this book the term "foreman" is applied to any individual who has supervisory responsibilities whether over one person or a group. This title probably designates the largest group of supervisors in industry and certainly defines a common area of responsibilities, even though the specific responsibilities of individual foremen may vary.

Three Roles of the Foreman

Foremanship is the process of implementing management's planning by organizing a work group and a work plan to achieve management's objectives. This process divides the foreman's job into three important roles. When overseeing the group and its output, he is a *supervisor;* when taking management's general plans, reducing them to plans for his department, and acting on them, he is a *manager;* and when hiring and training employees, he is an *instructor.*

Each of these three major divisions of the foreman's job should be carefully analyzed. But, before attempting an analysis, a distinction should be drawn between managerial and supervisory responsibilities. Very frequently these two are carried on at the same time, and the distinction is not always clear-cut.

All work that involves inspecting equipment, tools, materials, and so on is supervisory in nature. If the foreman notes that a machine is in need of a new part, acting as a manager he has the machine repaired at the proper time and with the least interruption in production flow. If, as a supervisor, he notes that the machine is overloaded and may break down if the careless operator continues to overload, he must become a manager to prevent further abuse of the equipment. He may act as an instructor in teaching the operator the proper use of the machine.

In his capacity as supervisor, a foreman should always be alert to conditions causing dissatisfaction among the employees; as a manager, he improves the conditions. Operating costs are constantly rising, and as a supervisor the foreman notes the areas where they can be reduced; as a manager, he devises and installs an improved method of doing the work. As a supervisor, the alert foreman sees many problems; what he does about them determines his effectiveness as a manager.

The foreman's job is to get out the work each day, check the progress of production, and maintain quality standards. He must always anticipate conditions which might arise. The time when things are running smoothly is not the time to relax and become complacent. Good executives know that this is when difficulties may be developing. Most men acquainted with safety programs have long since learned that many accidents result from nothing more than failure to recognize in advance the possibility of an accident. The foreman should see such safety hazards as machines running with guards off, goggles not being used, and badly stacked material; as manager, he should take the steps necessary to prevent an accident.

As a supervisor, the foreman should quickly detect any lowering of production rates in his department. There may be any number of causes—such as dissatisfaction or discontent among the employees, inaccurate measuring instruments, a drop in quantity or quality of material, equipment and machines in need of maintenance, or inadequately trained people. The foreman checks these factors and others to determine the cause of the decline in rate of production. In fact, as a supervisor he must constantly keep ahead of such developments to avoid lowered production rates or breakdowns.

The Foreman's Reluctance to Manage

Many foremen carry out the supervisory part of their jobs very well. They are constantly "on top of the job" and know when anything is going wrong. However, in some cases they do not act as managers and remedy the situations they see. Some foremen feel that their superiors do not want them to manage, that they should supervise and assume that someone else will manage. However, most enlightened top management people have long since learned that the supervisor–foreman who does not manage is of little value. No man can effectively use materials, machinery, men, and money by supervising alone. This idea of some foremen that they are not supposed to manage is often not really valid and is probably a rationalization on the part of those who do not know how to manage or do not want to manage. When foremen really *are not* allowed to manage, top management needs considerable soul searching and training to change the conditions which put the foremen in an untenable position. The foreman–manager must be responsible for planning and directing the activities of his department, improving methods, promoting and maintaining sound employer–employee relations, and reducing cost. He cannot and should not be held responsible unless he is permitted to—and does—manage the situation he sees as a supervisor.

As a manager, the foreman detects a decline in production, checks all elements, analyzes the causes, and takes steps to remedy them so that his output is maintained. If his orders now call for more man-hours than the shift will provide and overtime or increased staff is necessary, he gets approval and arranges for it. If he finds that his measuring devices have become inaccurate and cannot be adjusted, he arranges to have the defective instruments replaced. If he concludes that the decline in production rate is caused by some dissatisfaction among his employees, he proceeds to find out the specific cause of the dissatisfaction and removes it. In short, the foreman–manager analyzes situations and takes the steps necessary to insure that his department operates in the most effective manner.

The Foreman and "Climate"

One important aspect of the foreman's role as a manager is the development of the "climate" in his department. It was some years ago that the significance of climate, its effect on workers and on their productivity, gained recognition in the experiment at the Hawthorne plant of the Western Electric Company in Chicago. A team made up of men from the company and several professors from Harvard University attempted to determine what effect the introduction of new and varying working conditions would have on workers' productivity. First, a number of hand-picked operators known to be good performers were selected from various departments of the plant and put together to work as one group. Then changes in the working conditions were made. Rest periods were introduced, then taken away; illumination was increased and decreased; the work day was lengthened and shortened, none of these changes, however, adversely affected the workers' productivity. It remained high because, as the experimentors found later, of the experiment itself. This group of operators, especially selected, knew that attention was being paid them; they were part of something important; they wanted to cooperate.*

Much has been written—and learned—about the importance of climate since then, but it is still misunderstood in many quarters. Companies have tried all kinds of gimmicks and gadgets to compensate for what they lacked in good climate. And companies have become disillusioned when they found that their bright, new, shiny programs did not produce a more cooperative and productive group of people.

The establishment of the right climate is now considered an integral part of management in general and of the foreman's role as a manager in particular. A good foreman–manager is a man who generates a climate of growth, who feels responsible for the development of the men in his department. But there are many cases of foremen who block their subordinates' growth rather than encourage it. The kind of foreman who won't delegate authority and responsibility, who does not communicate even the minimal information the employee needs to do his job efficiently, and who does not show his people how to do a better job will fail utterly at his attempts to create a climate of growth.

The Foreman as Instructor

The third major element in the foreman's job is his role as a teacher. As he goes about his supervisory and managerial duties, he often finds that an employee either is not clear on what is ex-

---

* See F. J. Roethlisberger and W. J. Dickson, *Management and the Worker*, Harvard University Press, Cambridge, 1939.

pected of him or does not know how to do the work because he was not properly instructed. In some situations the employee believes he is doing a good job, but the foreman rates the employee's performance as only "fair." In other words, a gap exists that the foreman must close. So, if the foreman is to do his job completely, he must recognize this third role, that of instructor. He may not do the job of instruction himself; he may delegate all or part of it; but in any case he must see that the gap is closed.

The foreman–instructor must know the basic ingredients that make up the special skill of teaching a job. In delegating instructional work to others, he must be certain that they are not only good mechanics or operators but good instructors as well. In addition, the foreman must know which employees need training and what the teaching requirements of each particular job are. This teaching responsibility applies to apprentices, new employees, people transferred to the department, and, most important, the foreman's own understudy.

A particularly important part of the instruction task is the induction of the new employee to the work environment. In this phase of his job, the foreman must explain company policies, plant rules, and safety rules so that the employee understands what they are and what the reasons for them are. At the same time the new hire must be made to feel at home. The by-product of a good induction job is a good relationship between the foreman and the new employee from the outset.

The foreman, in short, has many specific duties and responsibilities. Some of these can be delegated, some cannot be delegated, and still others can be shared. To break down each of the numerous elements of foremanship in accordance with these degrees of delegation and, further, their classification as managerial, supervisory, or instructional may make an already difficult function seem more complex. Nevertheless, every foreman should be reasonably familiar with this breakdown. To help visualize it, Exhibit 1 charts most of the principal duties and responsibilities and classifies each.

Exhibit 1 shows how difficult it is to draw a clear, sharp line between classifications, especially in designating a duty as supervisory, managerial, or instructional. With few exceptions, any one item can and frequently does fall largely in one classification with an overlap into another. Certainly, where a duty may be fully dele-

Exhibit 1

The Foreman's Duties and Responsibilities

> **Legend**
> D—Can be delegated   S—Foreman as a supervisor.
> N—Cannot be delegated   M—Foreman as a manager
> O—May be shared with others   I—Foreman as an instructor

	Degree of Delegation			Role of the Foreman		
	D	N	O	S	M	I
1. Economically using and placing materials	X				X	
2. Hiring the right person for the job		X			X	
3. Controlling attendance: absence and lateness		X		X		
4. Preventing accidents			X	X		
5. Writing and submitting accident reports	X				X	
6. Adjusting grievances		X			X	
7. Improving morale of the workforce		X		X		
8. Maintaining discipline		X		X		
9. Keeping workers informed		X				X
10. Controlling false rumors		X		X		
11. Settling differences among workers		X		X		X
12. Keeping records and making reports	X				X	
13. Maintaining health and sanitation regulations	X			X		
14. Handling workers' compensation matters		X			X	
15. Planning and scheduling production		X			X	
16. Maintaining quantity of production			X	X	X	
17. Maintaining quality of production			X	X	X	
18. Improving work or production methods		X			X	
19. Keeping costs down			X		X	
20. Training workers			X			X
21. Requisitioning tools, equipment, and materials		X			X	
22. Inspecting and caring for tools and equipment	X			X		
23. Cooperating with other supervisors and units		X			X	
24. Promoting teamwork and cooperation			X	X		
25. Keeping employees' time records	X			X		
26. Reporting to operating officials on conditions needing attention		X			X	
27. Maintaining good housekeeping on the job	X			X		
28. Maintaining an adequate workforce		X			X	
29. Taking an interest in the employees		X		X		
30. Maintaining good public contacts		X			X	

gated, some initial instruction must be given. Nevertheless, if this subdivision is at all correct, of the 30 items making up the list—

  7 may be fully delegated.
17 may not be delegated.
  6 may be shared by others.

Again:

14 are largely supervisory.
16 are largely managerial.
 3 are instructional.

It is interesting to note from these figures that more than half the foreman's job calls for him to be a manager and cannot be delegated. On the other hand, more than half the supervisory duties and responsibilities *can* be delegated in whole or in part. This means that the foreman's job today is heavily a management job. If the foreman shirks his management duties and responsibilities or is not permitted to act as a manager, he is doing something less than half his job.

2

SELECTION

MANPOWER IS the most variable factor in industry. Every company has available to it the same money markets, the same materials, and the same equipment as its competitors. It may also have access to more or less the same people in the labor market. But these people can behave very differently after they have been hired. The difference between willing cooperation and apathetic "putting in time" can determine the success or failure of a company.

Since the foreman is the man who must get out the work, skillful management of manpower is primarily his job. He must have people who not only *can* but *will* produce. Selecting the right person for the job is a result of the combined efforts of the personnel department and the operating manager. But, in the final analysis, it is the foreman on the firing line who must make the selection. In many small companies where there is no personnel department, the foreman must do the entire job.

The Manpower Tripod

A good working group doing an above-average job must be based on a "manpower tripod"—a three-legged structure that will collapse if any one of the legs is weak, badly designed, or not firmly planted. The legs of the tripod are (1) selection, (2) training, and (3) motivation. Each leg is essential to good performance. A man who is well selected but inadequately trained will not be able to do a good job; a man who is a poor hiring risk may not respond to training; and a man who is not well motivated will not perform at capacity even if he has been carefully selected and well trained.

Hiring, training, and motivating are not completely separate, they are the three legs of a tripod. There is always some slight overlap between any two or all three of these activities in actual practice. Certainly when a person is being hired, some small amount of training or pretraining is also taking place; when a training program is in action, there must be some motivation to go with it. However, each is handled separately here for clarity.

Steps in Selection

Employees cannot be selected until job candidates appear from whom a choice may be made. Assuring an adequate "pool" of candidates will normally be the personnel department's responsibility, where one exists. But in a tight labor market, such as exists in most areas of the country, relatively few people will appear entirely on their own, "looking for a job," and most of those who do appear voluntarily will not make the best employees.

Step I—Recruiting. It is highly important in maintaining a proper recruitment effort for the foreman, by his actions with his own group, to help sell the company as a good place of employment. Reputations do get around, especially in smaller industrial communities. People know, in general, those companies that are good places to work, as well as those to which they would apply only as a last resort. More than one man has waited for weeks to get a job with one company rather than another. A good company reputation is based on many factors, including considerate and intelligent reception of applications and applicants and friendly interviewing. These factors attract desirable people, generate goodwill, and together create the impressions which determine whether a company is looked upon favorably or unfavorably.

All parties concerned should know what the various job specifi-

cations are and what kinds of people are needed to fill them. Especially in small companies with no personnel department, the foreman must have some reasonably specific idea of the sort of man who
can best fill a particular job.

Almost every adult has, at one time or another, set out to buy a
piece of equipment for home use—for example, a washing machine
or a lawn mower. The following process is usually followed in
choosing the make and model.

1. Decide why the equipment is needed and how it will be
   used.
2. Determine what makes and models are available to meet
   the need.
3. Visit dealers and inspect the models each one has in stock.
4. Have the dealers demonstrate the models.
5. Check the reference material to determine quality and dependability.
6. Make the selection.

The foreman should follow a similar procedure when he hires a
new employee. Once he has a firm grasp of the job and its specifications, he must find out who is available to fill it. Here is a list of
suggested sources for the man who must do his own recruiting:

1. Present employees—by promotion.
2. Friends of employees.
3. Relatives of employees.
4. Former employees.
5. State employment service.
6. Fee-charging employment agencies.
7. High schools, business and trade schools, colleges.
8. Social service agencies—YMCA's, churches, ethnic groups,
   and so on.
9. Vendors and salesmen who call on the company.
10. Company salesmen who call on customers.
11. Rehabilitation organizations.
12. Fraternal organizations.
13. Overflow from other companies.
14. Persons displaced from companies moving out of area.

The following are important aids in the utilization of these sources.

1. Awards to company employees for referring people who are hired.
2. Distribution of circulars and booklets.
3. Summer work for students in cooperative work programs.
4. Advertisements in newspapers, magazines, trade papers.
5. Notices on company bulletin boards.
6. Advertising on company trucks.
7. Radio advertising.

As long as the current tight labor market continues—and it is likely to do so indefinitely—the foreman must be constantly on the alert for people who appear to be potentially good candidates for work in his department or in the company. He may notice a young man filling his tank in a gasoline station, a bellhop in a hotel, a new acquaintance, or a total stranger sitting next to him in a coffee shop. In any case, whenever or wherever this happens, the foreman must always be ready to "talk up" his company and even a specific job. He must be able to state the important factors, both positive and negative, yet put his best foot forward as any good salesman will. A casual conversation touched off by a chance meeting can easily produce a valuable new employee.

Step II—Reviewing the application. No matter who speaks to the candidate and has him fill out the application blank when he visits the company, the foreman must obviously interview anyone being considered for a place in his department.

In preparing for this interview with the candidate, it is essential that the employment application be carefully reviewed. This process will probably open up questions to be asked as part of the interview. Points that should be noted include:

1. The number of the applicant's previous jobs and the length of time each was held, as evidence of stability. The estimate of stability will also depend upon the kinds of jobs he has held and his reason for leaving each.
2. The kinds of experience which the application indicates as they relate to the duties of the job to be filled.
3. The applicant's upward progress in his jobs. Have his re-

sponsibilities increased, decreased, or remained the same? Has his pay increased?

4. The applicant's time on earlier jobs, expressed in month and year ("1966 to 1967" could mean anything from two months to two years of service). Are there any periods unaccounted for in the service record? If so, information about them should be sought.

5. The applicant's educational background. Is it all that is needed? Did he finish his courses? Was he awarded a diploma or a degree? If not, why not?

6. The applicant's hobbies or special schooling. Do they indicate what his interests are?

7. Why is the applicant looking for work at the present time?

8. Does the neatness, legibility, completeness, or coherence of the application tell anything about the applicant?

9. Is there any information on the application (education, family, hobbies, prior employment) which will help to establish rapport at the start of the interview?

Step III—Interviewing. When the personnel office recommends an applicant for an opening in the foreman's department, he has every right to believe that good screening techniques have eliminated much of the possibility of error in the choice of the candidate.

What, then, is the foreman's job in selection? What can he do that a skilled employment interviewer, with the help of tests and devices, has not done? Can he do any more than greet his prospective employee?

This portion of the foreman's total responsibility should not be approached differently from any other. He can and should make full use of the staff services available and rely on their expert and specialized judgment, but he cannot relinquish his responsibility for getting out the work of his department in the most efficient and effective way possible by hiring the person who not only *can* but *will* do the job.

The foreman has three functions to perform in an interview with an applicant: (1) to complete the evaluation process, (2) to give the applicant detailed information about the job, and (3) to establish the correct relationship between himself and his new employee at the outset.

Establishing a good relationship is extremely important. The new employee must start his work with the conviction that his foreman, the man to whom he is directly and solely accountable, selected him for the job. Furthermore, the foreman must always feel that he made his own choice; that no one else picked the new employee and handed him over. When the foreman's judgment is at stake, he will try harder to see that his judgment is sustained.

The employment interview is a vitally important tool in building and maintaining an effective workforce. This interview serves three specific purposes: (1) It appraises an applicant's qualifications, abilities, and characteristics and compares them with the elements, requirements, and potentials of the job under consideration; (2) it gives the applicant the necessary information about the specific job—working conditions, hours, pay, opportunities and hazards, employment benefits and services—that will enable him to decide whether the job is acceptable; and (3) it builds goodwill toward the company.

A good interview requires mutual cooperation and confidence. From start to finish, the foreman should build and maintain a positive relationship with the applicant. This can be accomplished if sufficient preparation is made for the interview.

The interview should be limited to the two persons involved—the foreman and the candidate—and should be free from distractions and interruptions. Only under these conditions can both parties concentrate on the business at hand. Also, the candidate will be less self-conscious and less reluctant to speak of personal matters in complete privacy. Telephone calls, and the coming and going of other people, will block free expression on the candidate's part, if not actually ruin any chance of the foreman's gaining his confidence.

Time is important. No one knows precisely how long an interview should take. Suffice it to say that a well-conducted employment interview should be skillfully paced. And, since a foreman is a busy person, it should be scheduled, if possible, for a portion of the day when the foreman can do justice to it. By the same token, the applicant should not have to wait for a long period. Having a definite appointment helps to bolster his self-esteem, which will in turn tend to make him more receptive and cooperative.

If an unexpected emergency arises and an applicant does have to wait, he should be given something to do which has some bearing on the job, the department, or the company. Many companies have reading matter available—for example, trade publications, the company magazine, or the employee handbook. Exhibits of company products and pictures of its plants are also helpful.

Interviewing, like any other skill, can be learned only by doing. However, the time necessary to become a skilled interviewer may be shortened considerably by learning the right way from the start. Certain rules of interviewing have become generally accepted as good guides, particularly for the foreman.

These points should be considered before starting the interview.

1. The foreman should know in advance just what he wishes to determine and *can* determine.
2. He should beware of his own prejudices, impressions, and beliefs. Often the following fallacies are expressed:
   - "He certainly does look intelligent. We ought to staff the place with people like him."
   - "When you find a redhead, look out for a real temper."
   - "Watch out for the man with a shifty look about the eyes."
   - "It's risky to hire fat men; they're all lazy."
   - "The man who has lots of education is bound to be general-manager material."
   - "All athletes have strong backs and weak minds."
   - "The man who finds mathematics difficult cannot do *any* difficult job."
   - "Good handwriting indicates brains."
   - "This fellow talks very well. Put him on that really tough job."
   - "Look at all the technical courses he took! He should be a good engineer."
3. In addition to routine questions about trade or profession, develop others that require real *thinking* to arrive at the correct response.
4. Do not be overinfluenced by first impressions.
5. Avoid these mistakes during the actual interview:
   - Feet-on-the-desk pose.
   - Stuffed-shirt attitude.
   - Third-degree approach.
   - Trick questions.

- Making promises that may not or cannot be kept. Don't oversell.
- Overqualifying—selecting someone far above the job in ability.
- Talking too much.
- Expressing opinions.
- Making notes during the interview.
- Placing words in the candidate's mouth.
- Giving the applicant the impression that you are doing him a favor by giving him some of your valuable time.
- Being late or unavailable for a scheduled interview.

The foreman should begin the interview informally on a subject which he knows (from the application) is of interest to the applicant. This puts the applicant at ease and helps open the door for securing more specific information. It should always be kept in mind, however, that the interview is a business situation and not a purely social contact. As soon as the applicant seems to be talking freely and naturally, the foreman should direct the conversation toward the topics which must be covered to evaluate the applicant's fitness for the job. The foreman must always be in control of the interview and keep it moving in the proper direction.

Every effort should be made to move smoothly from one topic of conversation to another. Sudden changes can put the applicant on the defensive; he may feel that an attempt is being made to trick him. The foreman should not try to impress the applicant with his vocabulary, but should talk at a level at which the applicant feels comfortable. By talking over the applicant's head, the foreman will only build an invisible wall between the applicant and himself.

Questions designed to gain information or to clarify a statement must be asked in any interview. Leading or suggestive questions should be avoided; they usually elicit inaccurate responses. If the foreman asks, "Do you think what I have told you about the job sounds interesting?" he will probably get an affirmative answer, whether the applicant feels that way or not. If instead he asks, "How do you feel about the job?" the applicant is more likely to state his true feelings.

A few recommendations on the questioning technique follow:

Start with questions least likely to cause the applicant to back off. There may be "touchy" questions later which he will resist less if the atmosphere is favorable.

Ask questions that cannot be answered with an unqualified yes or no and thus gain valuable data in expanded answers.

Avoid trick questions. The foreman should not want or need to trap the candidate.

Keep questions to a minimum and ask them one at a time. If the applicant seems confused, it may be because of too many rapid-fire questions. On the other hand, if the foreman finds himself doing all the talking, more questions may be needed.

Interpret the applicant's answers as they are received; they may lead to other important questions.

Finally, the information obtained must be evaluated in terms of job needs. It is wise, after the interview has been completed, to write down enough facts to provide a picture of the applicant's background.

A suggested interview guide and observation form is presented in Exhibit 2.

A skilled interviewer knows that the session should be ended gracefully when—

1. He has discovered a definite reason to disqualify the applicant.
2. He has enough information for a final decision.
3. He has as much information as he can obtain at this stage and wishes to review it prior to an additional interview.

In closing the interview, certain procedures should be kept in mind:

1. If the foreman does not want to hire the applicant, he should tell him so. He can tell the applicant the basis for his disqualification if this information will benefit him.
2. If the foreman wants to hire the applicant, he should tell him so and sell him the job.
3. The foreman should make no promises to the applicant unless he is certain they will be kept.

4. If a final decision cannot be made, the applicant should be told that he will be notified by telephone or by letter by a specific date. The foreman should be certain that the applicant does not assume that he has definitely been offered a job if this is not the case.

Whatever the outcome of the interview, the foreman should close it with a smile, a handshake, and a "thank you." The applicant should feel on leaving that he has had an intelligent, sympathetic, and pleasant hearing and that the company is a good one to work for. The foreman should realize that he is dealing not only with an applicant for a job, but with a potential or actual customer or one who may influence a customer.

The 16 points that follow constitute a general summary of the

---

Exhibit 2

Suggested Interview Guide

Name _____ Date _____ Interviewer _____

1. Education
    a. College or special training.
    b. Specialty in school (useful to this company).
    c. Best subjects and grades.
    d. Poorest subjects and grades.
    e. Extracurricular activities.
    f. Special achievements.
    g. Method of financing education.
    h. Organizations (honorary, professional, social).
2. Work Experience
    a. Duties.
    b. Likes and dislikes.
    c. Achievements—things done well or less than well.
    d. Working conditions.
    e. Number of jobs.
    f. Reasons for changing jobs.
    g. Leadership experience.
    h. Factors of job satisfaction.
    i. Experience transferable to this company.
    j. Total job accomplishment.

principles of interviewing. Exhibit 3 is a pattern for an interview, illustrating the foreman's dual role of participant and observer.

1. Have adequate background information on the man. Be familiar with the application form. Contact other sources, such as previous interviewers, if any.
2. Know the judgments which will have to be made.
3. Hold the interview in private.
4. Distinguish between *description* and *evaluation*. Do not attempt to evaluate prematurely.
5. Put the applicant at ease. Be really interested in him.

Exhibit 2 (*continued*)

3. Present Social Adjustment
   a. Interests and hobbies.
   b. Marital status.
   c. Spouse's interests and personality. Relocation?
   d. Interest in family—children or other dependents.
   e. Financial stability—housing, insurance, and so on.
   f. Health status.
4. Positions Desired
   a. Type of work interested in.
   b. Reasons for interest.

Interviewer's Observations

Name _____ Date _____
1. Observations on total school achievement.

2. Observations on total work experience.

3. Observations on present social adjustment.

4. Positions desired.

   a. Type of work interested in.

   b. Reasons.

5. General observations (Elaboration of rating and recommendation)

6. Job offer?

   Yes, definitely ☐ Yes ☐ No ☐ For (job) _____

6. Conduct a *conversation,* not an *inquisition.*
7. Phrase questions properly in each area.
   a. Ask for a narrative statement of previous jobs which have demonstrated certain sought-after qualities rather than a mere chronological statement of experience.
   b. Use "open" questions. To get extended answers, start with the words "how," "what," "when," "where," "which," or "why."
   c. Unless a yes or no answer is required, avoid beginning questions with the words "can," "do," "is," "are," "will," or "shall."
8. Be a good listener—let the applicant talk, but direct the conversation unobtrusively.
9. Maintain control without appearing to do so.
10. Talk the applicant's language—don't talk down to him or in any way appear superior.
11. Distinguish between the factual content and the manner of its presentation.
12. Develop and use questions as informal tests of trade or professional-technical knowledge. Think of ways in which the knowledge, skills, and qualities the job requires may best be established within the limits of the interview.
13. Do not let the interview become mechanical; keep on the alert for unexpected evidence.
14. After the close of the formal part of the interview, watch for additional evidence. The applicant may be more relaxed and let his guard down. If convenient, take him to lunch; he may talk more freely.
15. Close the interview with the best present and future overall interests of the company in mind.
16. Record *facts* during the interview and *impressions* and *judgments* immediately thereafter. Do not trust memory.

Step IV—*Check prior employers.* Too much emphasis cannot be placed upon checking the references of all applicants. Usually the information furnished by applicants is correct, but it should still be verified. This involves checking with former employers to confirm dates of employment, positions held, pay rates, quality of service,

(*text continues on page 34*)

Exhibit 3

Pattern for an Interview

The Foreman's Role as Participant

Step I—Put the applicant at ease.
   Talk to him about his background.
   Show him you know how he feels.
   Watch for the point when he feels free to talk.
Step II—Get him to talk about himself.
   Ask broad questions.
   Ask what, why, when, where, who, how—*but not too close together.*
   Keep at a level he can handle.
   Give him time to think.
Step III—Steer him toward giving the needed information. Ask questions
   (or make statements) so he will tell you:
   What he knows.
   What he thinks.
   How he meets problems.
   What his attitude to a work situation is.
   If he bluffs or jumps to conclusions.
   If he analyzes, plans, organizes.
   If he is persuasive, dull, aggressive.
Step IV—Sum up—tell him how he stands.
   If you want to hire him:
   Sell him on the job, how he will fit in, and why you think so. But don't
     pressure him.
   If you don't want to hire him:
   Tell him so tactfully.
   If you don't know:
   Tell him so tactfully.

The Foreman's Role as Observer

Step I—Observe the applicant.
   What does he do with his face? Hands? How does he sit? Walk? Dress?
Step II—Interpret his actions—what do they mean?
   Is he nervous?
   Is he expressing a basic personality?
Step III—Evaluate him.
   His personality as an individual; as a part of the organization.
   His previous experiences. What did he do with them?
   His future promise. What are the possibilities for growth on the job?

reasons for leaving, and whether they would rehire the applicant. All these factors have an important bearing on the final selection of applicants.

If the company or plant has a central personnel office, it will undoubtedly have a form to use and may also get the necessary information. In smaller companies the foreman will have to do his own checking, and he should design a rough form for his own use.

The references to be checked are selected from the application. The best check is a face-to-face conversation with the prior employer. However, this is too time-consuming for any foreman. The poorest way to check is to mail the form to the prior employer and ask him to complete and return it. In 50 percent of the cases the form will not be returned, or, if it is, it will not be entirely reliable. The easiest and most effective way to check is by telephone. The person making the call should be just as attentive to what the person on the other end does *not* say and the *tone* of his response as to what is actually said. It is best to call the prior supervisor of the applicant. If he can be reached, he can and frequently will give more information about the applicant than an employee in the personnel office who is reading from a card.

After the calls are made to each of the recent employers, the information should be documented and filed for reference.

What About Testing?

In spite of comprehensive application forms, exhaustive interviews by skilled people, and thorough checking with prior employers and others, an applicant may still need to demonstrate his vocational ability. Therefore, to determine a prospect's ability and to make selections more accurate, some companies make use of tests of various kinds. Oral questions and answers about tools and materials are common tests used by foremen. Others are paper and pencil tests of diagrams and designs of tools and materials that are to be recognized and named by the applicant, terms to be explained, or problems to be worked out. These are usually used for practical trade jobs, such as ordinary shop work involving the use of blueprints, tools, equipment, and materials. There are also tests for strength, mental alertness, and intelligence and tests for special abilities in spelling, vocabulary, figure checking, computation, and reasoning.

Most tests are set up as records to be attached to the application. The special requirements of a particular company, its size, and the skills it needs in its employees all help to decide what kinds of tests to adopt. Whatever these methods and tests are, they should be selected after careful study and experimentation and then used only when there seems to be no other way to determine some characteristic which is important to the job. When the tests are decided upon, only qualified persons should administer, score, and interpret them.

Tests are not 100 percent foolproof, nor are they infallible. They are much better at predicting failure than they are at predicting success. They should therefore be used as an *aid* in selection and should never replace the judgment of the foreman. The results of tests should not carry more than 20 percent of the total weight of considered elements. On the other hand, the foreman should not oppose tests—which, if properly used, can be a great asset to him and to the organization.

In any organization, finding the right person for the job will always depend upon personal appraisal by the foreman or supervisor. If the foreman has an intelligent understanding of the many important factors involved, he will do his level best to get the right person for the job from the very beginning and in that way reduce many of his present costly headaches.

3

TRAINING

One of the major responsibilities of supervisory personnel is to help people adjust themselves to their jobs so as to benefit both themselves and the organization. This involves adjustments on two sides—fitting the job to the worker and the worker to the job.

For example, consider the familiar situation of the young man going into some branch of the armed forces. He must adjust himself to the physical routine involved and learn many rules and procedures foreign to his usual line of thought and action. Above all, he must learn to get along with his superiors and with his fellow men. The individual who can make this physical, mental, and social adjustment will be a happier, more efficient, and more effective member of the military establishment.

Much the same adjustment must be made by the new employee. Between the time he is hired and the time he becomes a contented, effective producer, there is a period of adjustment. The first phase of training (induction) is designed to convert the recruit into an employee. In this process, the foreman should try to get across certain information, reduce any fears or uncertainties about the new job, and make the new employee feel at home.

First Impressions

The foreman should first of all be tolerant and sympathetic. He must remember that in his own early days on a new job he, too, had many questions, some of which he kept to himself, but his foreman anticipated them in any case. He may also remember that his first foreman did not try to make himself a "big shot," an admirable quality. In the long run, the impression which the new man forms of the foreman, the shop, and the organization on that important first day is going to be lasting and should be the finest possible. The foreman can do more at the outset in creating the right kind of relationship than he can in all the weeks that may follow. He should be friendly toward the new employee, who will then go home with a much happier outlook and a kind word for the management among his friends.

As first impressions are most important, the foreman should not let a newly employed person stand around waiting for something to do. It will make him uneasy and distract the other employees. A better practice is for the foreman to give the new employee a personal welcome, address him by name, and tell him who his supervisor is, what the main job of the department is, and who the others in the group are. The new employee should be introduced to all the members of his work group. He needs to know the timekeeping procedure and the location of the lockers, the washroom, and the lunchroom or cafeteria. It is often a good idea to assign one of the older employees to eat lunch with the new man on his first day. If there are special departmental rules or safety rules, he should be instructed in them immediately. The foreman should sell the new employee on the need for the rules and their benefit to him so that the new employee will think of the company as a good place to work. The supervisor should give the new man every opportunity to ask questions. No matter how good a job of explaining may have been done, he probably has questions. There will never be a better chance to get them off his chest. It is important to make the new man feel that his questions are always welcome. If the line of communication to the foreman is direct and open at all times, questions can be answered and problems can be resolved before they fester into complaints and grievances, as they surely will if they are not dealt with early. Every foreman should want his people to look to him for the answers and not to the "locker-room lawyer."

And there are other features of the new organization about which the new employee will want to know. Most companies these days have a host of fringe benefits which will need explaining even if they are in printed form. Therefore, it is obvious that all the points to be covered in any induction program cannot be communicated to an employee at one time. In fact, most of them will be taken up in short discussion periods, allowing the learner time in between to digest what has been discussed. The first day or part of a day will probably touch on only the highlights, giving just enough information to get the new man started and make him feel at home on the job. Details (information about fringe benefits, for example) can be filled in later.

A Typical Schedule

A complete induction program should probably be spread over several weeks while the new employee is learning the techniques of the job. This approach has the added advantage of bringing the foreman and his new employee into more frequent personal contact, allowing them to build up a good working relationship.

While most induction is carried on in informal conferences between the individual employee and the foreman, there are times when group induction is practical. When a number of employees join a department at the same time, as they do in peak periods, it is customary to meet them as a group for their first induction session. This not only saves time and assures everyone of getting the information in the same way, but also helps to get everyone acquainted. However, subsequent sessions should be conducted separately, so that the foreman can get to know each person and can adjust his information to individual needs.

Despite all that has been said about the need for good induction, nothing much can happen until the induction program is set down on paper in terms of *what* is to be done, *when* it is to be done, and *by whom* it is to be done. The first portion of the induction program to be spelled out by the foreman includes five essential steps to be followed as outlined:

Step 1. Make a friendly first impression.
    a. Smile.
    b. Tell him your name and get his.
    c. Show interest in him by asking friendly questions (about his hobbies, for example).
    d. Express a sincere desire to help him make good.
    e. Tell him you welcome questions.
Step 2. Explain the pay system.
    a. Tell him what his pay rate is.
    b. Explain how his pay is computed.
    c. Tell him when he will be paid.
    d. Explain overtime, holiday, shift premium rates.
    e. Show him how he can improve his earnings.
    f. Answer any pay questions that arise.
Step 3. Explain important rules and regulations.
    a. List general safety rules.
    b. List working rules.
    c. Explain notification of absence procedure—be specific.
    d. Provide passes, badges, identification.
    e. List restricted areas.
    f. Explain plant protection regulations.
Step 4. Tell him about employment services and opportunities (sell him on the future of his job).
    a. Tell him about the vacation plan—amount and how to qualify.
    b. List the medical and health services.
    c. Mention the recreational activities.
    d. Advise him of the educational opportunities.
    e. Explain the promotional opportunities.
    f. Explain the group insurance.
Step 5. Acquaint him with places and fellow workers.
    a. Show him the first-aid room or stations.
    b. Show him the washroom.
    c. Make sure he knows where dressing and locker rooms are.
    d. Show him stockroom, stores, and supplies.
    e. Show him the time clock.
    f. Tell him where the cafeteria is.

A simple induction schedule is shown in Exhibit 4.

Exhibit 4

Suggested Induction Schedule

FIRST DAY

1. On arrival at work location.	Report to foreman. a. Introduction to president or top manager in plant or department. b. Brief history of company and its objectives by foreman.
2. Immediately after No. 1.	Information needed in daily routine. a. Locker room facilities. b. How to get to and from work, parking, and so on. c. Starting time, meal periods, stopping time. d. Hours per week, overtime, recording hours worked. e. When, where, and how employee will be paid. f. Opportunity for questions.
3. Following No. 2.	Meeting other workers, getting to know layout of work area. a. Trip through department with explanation of function. b. Introduction to workplace and work group. c. Location of bulletin boards, rest room, washroom. d. Special rules on leaving job or department, smoking, safety.
4. Following No. 3 until lunch period.	Job instruction—under close supervision.
5. Lunch period.	Lunch with someone from the department and introduction to other employees.
6. One-half hour before end of workday.	Discussion on how employee is getting along; informal conversation about himself, family, hobbies, and other personal matters.

Exhibit 4 (*continued*)

SECOND DAY

7. When convenient.	Discussion about other basic procedures and policies. a. When and whom to call when late or absent. b. Reporting accidents. First aid. c. Housekeeping and sanitation rules. d. General safety rules.

FIRST WEEK

8. When convenient.	Review of additional policies. a. Vacations, holidays, leaves of absence. b. Union contract provisions (if any). c. Promotions. d. Trips to other departments.
9. At end of week.	Interview with employee. a. Discussion on what he thinks of the job. b. Clarification of any misunderstanding.
10. At time he gets first pay check.	Explanation of pay check. Answers to questions on deductions, overtime, and so on (by foreman or office manager).
11. At later date.	Follow-up. Explanation of group insurance (by foreman or office manager).

Every organization wants satisfied employees who know their jobs and think intelligently while on the job. The responsibility for employee satisfaction lies primarily with the foreman, and the more skilled he becomes as a teacher the greater will be his chances for accomplishing the desired results.

Training is a teaching process which goes on between two—or more—people and requires the cooperation of both. Training is not something to be done at odd moments or in an emergency; it should be continuous and be conducive to growth on the part of the employee. The goal is to pass along, not just information, but a new way of doing things.

John Ruskin said, "Education does not mean teaching people what they do not know. It means teaching them to behave as they do not behave. . . . It is a painful, continual, and difficult work to be done by kindness, by watching, by warning, by precept, and by praise, but above all—by example." Those last two words are important, for the foreman produces his most permanent impressions by example.

On-the-job instruction should be done well—best of all, by someone who not only knows the job but also has the ability to pass along that knowledge. Many adults know arithmetic very well but have difficulty in teaching the subject to their children. The ultimate objective is to get the new employee or an old employee on a new job to do the work correctly, quickly, and conscientiously and to form the right work habits.

Over the years a number of methods have been used to teach jobs. One that is still frequently used is to place the new man with an experienced worker. This is a good method if the experienced worker has the right attitude toward the company and knows how to instruct, although it somewhat dilutes the employee-foreman relationship. Some companies have staff instructors in "vestibule" schools—that is, training sessions led by qualified instructors in which the new employee spends days or weeks away from the workplace learning the job until he is proficient enough to be placed in the production line. Because of the expense involved and the large number of participants required to break even financially, this method is limited to large organizations. A third method—which is hardly worth calling a method—is to let the new man pick up the information himself in any way he can. This method usually results in his doing the job the wrong way because there are *many* wrong ways of doing anything and only *one* right way.

The fourth and best method is instruction by the foreman or supervisor. He is the one man who knows—should know—all the jobs and how he wants them done. Clearly he is in the ideal position to implant good work habits and attitudes.

People learn skills by seeing, hearing, and doing. A person never learned to swim by simply watching someone else swim or hearing a lecture on swimming. These two important elements of instruction must be followed by practice. It is a common mistake in industry to think that because a person has been told, he has been instructed. This belief is almost as silly as that of the foreman "who has no time" to teach his people. This is probably true, in his case, because he is busy correcting mistakes which should not and would not have occurred if the proper training had been done initially. Studies indicate that a person remembers—

10 to 15 percent of what he hears.
15 to 30 percent of what he hears and sees.
30 to 50 percent of what he himself says.
50 to 75 percent of what he does.
More than 75 percent of what he does with proper instruction.

Teaching on the job accounts for a sizable portion of the foreman's responsibility because of the following day-to-day situations and problems:

1. Turnover in a department, even though low, requires training new employees.
2. There are promotions and transfers into and out of the department.
3. New products are introduced or old products are changed.
4. New equipment is introduced.
5. New sales plans and campaigns are started.
6. Employee weaknesses and errors must be corrected.

The supervisor who does not know how to instruct is usually not an effective teacher for one or more of the following reasons:

1. He teaches his job in the order in which *he* performs it without realizing that a new employee may not necessarily learn in the same order and can become confused by an arbitrary sequence of tasks. A good instructor knows how to organize the information into the proper learning order.
2. Because he is an experienced worker, the supervisor may think of this job in *bigger units* than the new man can easily digest. A trained instructor knows how to break down the job into units of a size which the learner can handle.

3. Many supervisors assume that the learner knows as much as they do. Thus they may leave out important connecting links in their explanations.
4. The untrained supervisor stresses the things that seem important to *him,* not the things that are important when the job is being done by a beginner.
5. The supervisor does not explain *why* a task is done a certain way; thereby, it makes the job seem dry and dull and slows up learning.
6. The supervisor who is used to doing rather than teaching is likely to become impatient with someone who fails to learn quickly and assume the learner is slow or stupid.
7. The supervisor does not properly prepare himself before beginning instruction. Consequently, he may not have a clear idea of the exact number of steps in the operation and is likely to backtrack, get the sequence mixed up, or forget what he wanted to say. This behavior causes him to hesitate, and the new worker assumes that he does not know his job very well.
8. The untrained instructor may lack a full understanding of human relations and may therefore antagonize the learner without knowing it. A good instructor knows how to gain the confidence, goodwill, and cooperation of the learner.

For all these reasons an untrained instructor may find that his men take longer to attain top performance, or they may learn the job the wrong way and then require more of the supervisor's time for correction. What is more, his men may develop resentments which show in their performance and could spread to others.

In contrast, a good instructor knows his job first of all. He uses the best methods and work habits. No man can teach someone else to do a job well if he is just a dub at it himself. Over and above this qualification, however, a good instructor—

1. Puts himself in a new employee's place and thinks back to the time when he, too, was a learner.
2. Has the patience to stay with the new man and gain his confidence and respect. This is half the job; if it can be done, the rest will be easy.
3. Never makes anything look hard.

4. Never discourages the new worker by getting angry or impatient or by implying that he is a slow learner.
5. Is sincerely interested in seeing the new man get on. Answers all questions, no matter how simple, because the kinds of questions asked show whether the instruction is effective or whether a new approach is needed.
6. Never loses self-control in handling the new man. Once the instructor loses the new employee's respect, he has lost his usefulness so far as that particular man is concerned.
7. Can picture his job as a series of simple steps rather than as a complicated whole.
8. Can size up men and understand them.
9. Understands the simple principles of instruction outlined in this chapter.

The Instruction Process

Before any instruction can be given, the following preliminary steps must be taken:

1. *Prepare a job breakdown.* (See Exhibit 5.) This procedure picks out the important steps and key points in the job. Here the supervisor learns to select and stress those little knacks he knows so well that he may forget to mention them. These knacks have to be included in the training if the new employee is to do the job right and with reasonable speed.
2. *Prepare a training plan.* An organized training plan indicates how to spot an employee's immediate training needs and how to schedule the training to meet these needs. The plan should contain the essential parts of a job and show when and how training is to be done and by whom. This plan is especially helpful when training is spread over a longer period of time and covers more area than usual. The main point is to determine how much skill the worker has to have and by what date.
3. *Have everything ready.* If the job requires materials, supplies, and equipment, they must be ready before instruction starts. Lack of preparation on the supervisor's part will confuse the employee and waste time.

In the civilized parts of the world, most people know how to tie their shoelaces so well that they can do it with their eyes closed. However, if this skill had to be taught to some person who was wholly unfamiliar with shoes, it might be quite difficult. Exhibit 5 presents a breakdown of this small task.

A glance at the job breakdown should help in the preparation of

Exhibit 5

How to Tie a Shoe

LEFT HAND

RIGHT HAND

1. Grasp left shoelace; do the same as right hand.

1. Grasp right shoelace between thumb and forefinger about two inches above top eyelet of shoe. Pull tight.

2. Cross shoelaces, keeping right one in front or on top, using third or fourth finger of each hand to pull laces across each other (both hands at same time).

3. Push left thumb through laces, using left forefinger to pull left lace through to form knot.

3. Grasp left lace between right thumb and forefinger.

4. Slide left hand to left away from knot, at the same time pull down on right lace.

4. Pull down on left lace until knot forms on shoe tongue in line with top eyelet holes.

5. Catch left lace (now on right side) between left thumb and forefinger just at knot; slide along about one inch. Hold end of right lace around fifth finger at same time.

5. Hold left lace between thumb and forefinger, about two inches from end and bring down to form bow.

6. Bring right lace up in front, over bow, and over right forefinger.

6. Hold bow while performing Step 6 with left hand.

7. With left thumb, push right lace through hole made by right forefinger.

7. Make hole with right forefinger.

8. Keep pushing through hole.

8. Grasp lace as it is pushed through between thumb and forefinger.

9. Grasp left bow (made by right lace) and pull down, tightening knot.

9. Pull through and down, tightening knot.

a training plan by indicating the degree of complexity of the job and helping the foreman determine whether the training must be spread over more than one lesson, where the cutoff points are, and even when and how some of the elements are to be taught. The breakdown should also indicate what materials, supplies, or equipment should be on hand before instruction starts to avoid confusion and waste of time.

Now that the foreman has prepared himself to teach, the first step in the actual instruction is the preparation of the person who is to receive the instruction—the employee.

Step 1—Prepare the employee. First, put him at ease. Even though the new man may have just been through a good induction program, he is now confronted with the actual job situation and he may again be somewhat apprehensive and nervous. It is therefore essential that he be put at ease about anything that may be worrying him. He may be anxious about how he and his foreman will get along, whether his performance will suit the foreman, or whether it will meet the company's expectations. The foreman should indicate by what he says and does that nothing unreasonable will be expected and that he is interested in making the job easy and effective. He should indicate that he is more interested in how well the new man will be doing several weeks from now than in how he responds immediately to the job situation.

Second, explain the job and its importance. It is essential that the new employee understand the importance of his job. When he sees the job as a vital part of the whole operation, he becomes more interested in learning to do it the right way.

Third, create interest. The foreman-teacher should never take it for granted that a man will be interested in learning the job just because he gets paid for doing it. The only way to be sure of his interest is to make him realize that it is to his personal advantage to learn to do, and do well, the tasks he is about to be taught. He will improve his skills and, thus, his ability to make a living. He will be able to do his work more easily and more effectively, which means progress and success for him.

The greater the new employee's interest, the easier will be the foreman's job of training.

Step 2—Present the job. At this point, the instructor actually begins to present the new material.

First, follow the job breakdown. Whenever the foreman trains an employee for a job, he should have the job breakdown with him and keep to it. This will insure his staying on the track and giving economical and efficient instruction.

Next tell, show, and illustrate one step at a time. There are many different ways in which the presentation can be made, none of which is as effective by itself as it is when used in combination with others.

The five senses—sight, hearing, touch, taste, and smell—are avenues through which impressions reach the brain. If an individual is to learn, he must use one or more of these senses. The most effective presentation, therefore, will bring the greatest number of these avenues into use.

Some of the best teaching the world has ever known was put across with simple illustrations or parables. When talking to a group of farmers, the Great Teacher used the parable of the farmer who went forth to plant seed—some falling on stony ground, some on fertile soil, and so on. He knew the value of an illustration that was within the experience of the group.

Illustrations are indeed a very effective means of presentation when they are well chosen and are understandable to the learner. They are even more effective when used in combination with a demonstration. On the other hand, an illustration is much less effective when it takes the place of a demonstration.

The learner must be told *why* the job is to be done and *why* it is to be done this way. Stick to key points; don't waste time on unimportant detail. A person's capacity to absorb and retain is limited. If the telling is cluttered with a lot of irrelevancies, that just makes it harder for the learner to retain the important facts.

Teach clearly, completely, and patiently—but not too much at one session. Tell the learner only what he can absorb—anything else is misleading and a waste of time.

Use language with which the employee is familiar. Every shop has its own terms—its own jargon—which everyone but the new employee understands. Avoid these terms or explain them if they must be used.

Whenever a learner watches the foreman do a job, he is watching to see *how well* it is done. The supervisor's demonstration always sets the standard and governs the quality of the work when the man is left alone.

Step 3—Try out the worker. Have him do the job. People learn by doing or applying what they have heard and seen. In addition, doing the job correctly builds self-confidence, which is essential at this stage for success.

Some foremen think that they should leave the new man at this point, saying they will be back shortly to see how he is getting along. These foremen claim that if they stay it will make the learner nervous and they do not have the *time* to stay.

On the other hand, there are certain disadvantages for both the foreman and the learner if the foreman leaves at this point. In the first place, the door is wide open for the learner to try "experiments," and no one will be present to prevent mistakes or to answer questions. Also, the foreman will not be able to check on his own presentation if he is not there to see what happens as the new man does the job. Therefore, it is strongly recommended that the foreman or whoever is the teacher remain with the learner.

Correct errors and omissions immediately. Keep the following points in mind:

1. Avoid criticism. Instead of bawling out a man for having done something wrong, show him how he could have done it a better way.
2. Compliment before correction. The new man must have done *something* well. When he is sincerely complimented first, he will be more receptive to correction.
3. Let the learner correct himself. This is the best way to eliminate unpleasantness. After the compliment, ask him if he can think of anything he could have done that would have made his performance even better. If he can't, of course, the foreman will have to make a suggestion.
4. Don't overdo correction. Too much fuss about every little thing may make a new worker nervous and damage his self-confidence.
5. Don't correct in front of others. This is the worst kind of criticism.
6. Don't be too quick to blame the learner. The fault may be with the teaching. Keep in mind that, if the employee has not learned, it is likely that the foreman has not taught.

Encourage the learner. To repeat: Compliments are important aids in building self-confidence and a feeling of success. Compliment freely, but don't overdo it. There must be a good basis for all compliments; mere flattery won't work. Improvement, progress, or even a good try that fails may provide the reason for a compliment—be prompt with it, don't wait until the next day.

Get feedback. The foreman-teacher must be sure that the learner can do the job exactly as the foreman did it, that he can repeat the instructions given him completely and accurately. This is of vital concern to the foreman, and one way to find out whether learning has actually taken place is for him to ask questions which can not be answered simply by yes or no. If the foreman asks his new man, "Do you understand?" or, "Do you see?" the answer invariably will be an affirmative nod or a yes. This reaction means nothing. The learner says yes for two very good reasons. He thinks he does understand, and he doesn't want to appear stupid or slow to his new boss. The foreman can easily be misled by such answers and continue to pour on more information when, in fact, the new man can not absorb any more.

On the other hand, if questions start with the word "who," "what," "how," "where," "when," or "why," the learner will indicate by his answers whether he understands. For example, the answer to the question, "What is it that you have seen me do?" or "Why do we feel that these steps are necessary?" will let the foreman know which points were not understood so that he can go over them until they are cleared up.

Step 4—Follow through. Put the new man on his own. After he has shown that he can do the job, he should be put on his own so that he can become confident of his own ability.

Encourage questions. The foreman should make it clear that asking questions is not looked upon as a sign of weakness. No matter how simple the question may appear, it should be treated seriously and with respect. This attitude will teach the new employee to come to his supervisor with questions or problems at any time.

Check frequently. The foreman should monitor the performance of his new man as often as seems necessary but less and less frequently as proficiency increases. There should never be an abrupt withdrawal.

Let the employee know how he is doing. If the new man is doing the job the way the foreman wants it done, he should be praised. If he gets off the beam, he should be told so constructively. Errors never eliminate themselves. It is the foreman's responsibility to let the new man know when he is doing the job correctly and where he may need to improve. If the right man was hired for the job in the first place, he will *want* to know how he is doing.

Summary

As has been said, the primary responsibility of the foreman is to teach his employees the one best way to do the job. This of course assumes that the foreman has the ability to put across ideas in a systematic and effective manner. In American industry, about 75 percent of foremen consider teaching the most difficult part of the job, and a large percentage delegate teaching to others or let the new man "get it" as best he can. Maintenance foremen in small shops often are overworked and exhausted because they would rather do the job themselves than teach it to another man. This practice of no training makes heavy demands upon the foreman's time and energy in the form of correcting mistakes, controlling scrap, and worrying about the many things left undone.

Learning how to instruct becomes of primary importance to the foreman himself if he is to attain worthwhile results from the energy he puts into his job. The coin has two sides: He must not only become familiar with the techniques of putting ideas across but be able to select the ideas that must be put across. The technique of teaching a job and the procedure for determining what to teach have been presented in this chapter. But it is not enough to read about it; as stated, no skill is ever developed without the third element of doing it. The axiom "Practice makes perfect" applies to the foreman-teacher as well as to his employees.

4

MOTIVATION

A SHORT TIME AGO, a large group of middle and top managers was asked the question, "What is the major problem in your job?" The many answers were expressed in a variety of ways, but well over 50 percent of the group responded, in effect, "Getting my people to do what I want done in the proper way and at the right time." These managers were saying that, with all their communication skills, they lacked sufficient knowledge of what it takes to motivate their employees to act as desired.

People constitute an unlimited potential force in business and industry. A machine has a rated capacity beyond which it cannot go no matter how much physical energy is applied to it: It can produce only so much and no more. But, there is no practical limit to what people can accomplish when they are motivated to do so. Only because of this potential has man advanced from a subsistence level to the highest standard of living the world has ever known. Motivated manpower produces "heartpower" (favorable attitudes) and "brainpower" (judgment and creativity). Any foreman should prefer these human powers to more physical energy (commonly known as horsepower) from his people.

There is a tremendous difference between the people who work harder by applying more physical energy to their jobs and those who work creatively to develop more productive and satisfying ways of doing things. Working harder results in a limited increase in output and may produce a decrease in satisfaction. Even if the amount of physical energy applied could be doubled and thus cause a man to work twice as hard, his productivity would not rise by any phenomenally large amount. In the early days of scientific management, the results of the "work harder" approach were known to be limited and, in many respects, quite negative. Today we know that the "work creatively" approach, in contrast, provides personal satisfaction and offers unlimited opportunities for progress. The "work smarter, not harder" strategy means that the foreman must get everyone into the act instead of confining the efforts of his people to merely carrying out orders which he or someone else has developed.

Motivation is a very complex subject to a student of psychology. However, when boiled down for practical use on the job by the foreman, it need not be as complex. In the first place, "motivation" is defined as "that which moves or induces a person to act in a certain way." It is an inner drive—something internal which causes a person to do something. It is certainly not a process of inducing people to act against their own interest; that is manipulation, and people recognize it early in the game and cease responding to it.

An incentive, on the other hand, is the outside stimulus that encourages a person to take action. When presented to the employee by his foreman, incentive causes the employee to transform his inner drive or motive into specific behavior. An ugly example might be used to illustrate this point: A man steals a substantial sum of money; greed was his motive for stealing, and the money was the incentive which transformed greed into the theft. The motive of greed could well have remained in a dormant state forever, had not the incentive been placed before the man.

The next step is to determine the basic set of inner drives that motivate people on the job. Theories range from single needs (for example, Freud: All human behavior is motivated by the sex drive or some aspect of sex need; or Adler: All human behavior is motivated by the need to feel important) to multiple-needs theories with lists totaling from 25 or so to more than 100. The former are too simple to be used by the foreman; the latter are too complex.

The Maslow Theory

One usable theory was developed in 1943 by Dr. A. H. Maslow, now of Brandeis University.[1] In applying Maslow's much-cited theory, a person should think about himself and his own motivation, not about how it might motivate other people. If the theory seems to mean something to him, he can make his own adaptation of it. Then, after he has tested his adaptation in terms of his own experiences— after he has studied his own actions in terms of the theory—then he may have the patience and the humility to take a look at the behavior of other people in terms of their probable needs. Understanding this theory may, in fact, help the supervisor in his relationships not only with his subordinates but with others in the organization and in his personal life as well.

Granted, motivation is a complex phenomenon that cannot be reduced to a static diagram. Nevertheless, for clarity and ease of understanding, Maslow sets up the first hypothesis as follows: All human needs can be classified under five headings, making a spectrum or a continuum of needs ranging from basic physical needs (primary needs) to more human and social needs (secondary needs), each with its own priority. These include—in ascending order—basic physiological needs; safety and security needs; attention, love, and affection needs; esteem and self-respect needs; and self-realization needs.

While it is important for management people to know what an employee's primary and secondary needs are, it is even more important to keep in mind the definite sequence of domination shown by the five "need levels." Only after No. 1 is quite well satisfied does No. 2 come into prominence; No. 3 will not dominate until the two previous levels have been reasonably well met, and so on up the line.

Basic physiological needs. These are of two types: (1) basic physiological or primary needs proper and (2) environmental or secondary needs.

Some of the very simple and basic physiological needs are for food, water, sleep, air to breathe, and a comfortable or satisfactory temperature. These needs are universal among all people, but they

[1] Abraham H. Maslow, *Motivation and Personality*, Harper & Brothers, New York, 1954.

vary somewhat in intensity. For example, some people need more sleep than others. Social practice also plays a large part. It is customary in our part of the world to eat three meals a day and bodies respond accordingly, whereas other people can exist very nicely on two or four meals.

The secondary needs are much less tangible since they are not physical needs but instead are mostly social. Developing as people mature, they include such social needs as self-esteem, sense of duty, and a sense of belonging. These are the needs which make life very complicated for the foreman because nearly any action he takes will affect them. From this fact follows the basic motivational principle that *management planning should consider the effect of the proposed plan on the secondary needs of employees.*

Safety and security needs. In a typical business or industrial situation the first level—basic needs— seldom dominates because it is quite well satisfied. The second level—safety—also is basic; it includes, not only safety from pain, discomfort, and injury, but also "security." Business and government have long recognized this need; and, to satisfy it, we now have workmen's compensation, unemployment insurance, seniority clauses, social security, collective bargaining, and so on. It is the need which gains great prominence in periods of layoff and unemployment. However, generally this need is quite satisfactorily met in a typical business and industrial environment.

Love, affection, and attention needs. Here again, these needs do not become important until the levels beneath them have been reasonably well met. As recently as a half-century ago, this third level had still not gained ascendency in America. Men often worked a normal week of 60 hours merely to feed a family of five and keep a roof over their heads. Times have changed, however, and the present standard of living is so high that there is considerably more emphasis on the human factors.

Some foremen and managers are inclined to treat this third level lightly or dismiss it completely by saying that since this level concerns social factors, it should be met primarily off the job. On the other hand, if the employees in a department sleep an average of 8 hours each night and spend 40 hours each week on the job, simple arithmetic indicates that they are spending between one-third and one-half of their waking hours at work. Therefore, since the department is composed of a group of people who make up a social environment, it is imperative that some of these social needs be met on the job.

Esteem and self-respect needs. Next in order of priority is the fourth level, the need for esteem and respect—for recognition and status both external and internal. All employees want to feel worthy and to be respected, but they also want to believe that others are worthy and to respect them, too. This level's requirement may be best expressed as "human dignity"; it recognizes that the whole person is being employed, not just his strength or his skill.

This is probably the need that dominates the industrial society of today. It has gained great prominence these days largely because the first three basic needs are already at least partly satisfied. On the other hand, the assembly line and mass production have tended to destroy or dilute human dignity in industry. The worker who, years ago, built all or most of the automobile body could satisfy the fourth-level needs more easily than the worker who today applies nuts to bolts as the assembly goes by on the line.

Self-realization needs. The fifth and last level is the need for accomplishment and achievement, or self-realization. This one is not quite as obvious as some of the others because most people are not concerned about it yet—they are still quite busy trying to satisfy Needs 3 and 4. Yet the fact that the need for self-realization influences all levels is borne out by the observation that most people choose occupations that they like and that provide certain satisfactions of accomplishment. Moreover, to the degree that this need for self-realization can be satisfied, people will work to attain management's productivity goals.

Self-realization requires a certain pattern of personality traits in a person:

1. A close relation to reality—seeing things as they are, not as one hopes they are or as one is afraid they may be.
2. Love for humanity.
3. Acceptance of self and others with a full awareness of one's own and others' personal weaknesses and limitations.
4. A fresh appreciation of everybody and everything.
5. A philosophical and unhostile sense of humor.
6. Creativity.

Three things, in short, should be kept in mind about the five levels of need and their relative priority:

1. The five levels of need come into an individual's consciousness and demand satisfaction in accordance with the priority as presented. For example, no individual can be concerned with the fourth level until the first three are reasonably and continuously satisfied.

2. At any given time in a person's life, all five needs are present, but one is always dominant and most powerful. The individual's first unsatisfied need in order of relative priority becomes his dominant need.

3. A critical change in a person's life or in the situation in which he finds himself may cause a shift of that person's dominant need.

The individual tries to satisfy the need that is dominant at any given time. Though his behavior may not seem logical to an observer, that behavior has a goal and a purpose. The term "motivation" refers to a dynamic process in which are involved the needs of the individual, the goals toward which he is directed, his behavior, and the energy released in the individual for the attainment of those goals. This energy tends to increase in direct proportion to the intensity of his needs.

It is important, too, to recognize that these five needs merge into each other and do not have sharp lines of demarcation. They are more like the seven colors (red, orange, yellow, green, blue, indigo, and violet) of the spectrum, which merge with each other so that no one can tell quite where yellow, for example, stops and green begins. Because of this overlap, the individual gains at least partial satisfaction of more than one need at a time, and the dominant need at any specific time may change within a relatively short period. The fact that all needs are present at all times, with only one dominant but subject to change, partially explains the complex and dynamic nature of human motivation.

Needs Satisfaction Today

In the American economy, it is safe to say that the first two need levels are well met for most of the working population. The efforts of organized labor, state and federal laws, and increasingly progressive management over the past half-century leave little to be satisfied in these areas for the American worker. The third level of need, too, is reasonably well satisfied. However, more of these third-level satisfactions are being achieved off the job than on. While recognizing that a small, well-knit group working as a team is more effective in attaining organizational goals, managers have been a little afraid that group effort might work against them and, therefore, have not used this area of satisfaction to full advantage. When a person's acceptance or social needs are frustrated and he resists direction and becomes uncooperative, managers too often classify him as a "troublemaker."

Unlike those of the first three levels, esteem needs are rarely satisfied for people in the lower ranks of a typical industrial organization. In the mass production industries, the commonly used method of scheduling and organizing the work practically ignores this important means of motivation and actually works against the satisfaction of these needs.

What has just been said about the esteem needs is equally true for the self-realization needs. The conditions under which the great mass of people work, greatly improved though these may be, afford very limited opportunity for the self-realization needs to find expression. They are there, although somewhat dormant, and do meet with some satisfaction in off-the-job activities. More than one man thwarted in this area in his industrial life has found fourth- and fifth-level satisfaction in outstanding leadership of organized labor.

Many managements that provide good wages, good conditions, and all kinds of fringe benefits wonder why productivity does not increase with wages. However, most of these typical rewards can be used to satisfy the employee's needs only after he is away from the job: Any monetary rewards in wages and fringes, beyond those that adequately satisfy the basic physiological and security needs, go for the satisfaction of the three highest levels in off-the-job pursuits. If management paid more attention to the satisfaction of these needs on the job, there might be less demand for higher wages and more fringe benefits.

What the Foreman Can Do

Since the need for esteem and self-respect is the one which the workers in many industries must satisfy away from the job, it might be well to consider what the foreman can do on the job to create more satisfaction for his people in this area.

Self-esteem has been defined as "proper respect for oneself." This neat definition forestalls any misconception that self-esteem implies excessive self-assurance or a feeling of superiority. "Proper" respect means that a person has evaluated himself fairly and has not assumed an attitude of superiority in so doing.

The employee who has a proper respect for himself faces his tasks with more courage and confidence than one who feels inferior. Because he feels that what he does is of some importance, he is willing to put more of himself into it. This effort is reflected in his output. Furthermore, he carries on his duties in a cheerful, optimistic spirit which makes for pleasant relationships in the department. He has more sympathy for those who need help and is less prone to criticize. It is a basic part of the foreman's responsibility to build up, not to destroy, this self-esteem.

A foreman builds up employee self-esteem through a succession of considerate acts which are small in themselves but, in the aggregate, mean a lot to the employee. Suggestions as to the kinds of acts that build up employee self-esteem are listed under the "Do's" in Exhibit 6.

Care must be taken in this process to be sincere and to consider the individual case. Indiscriminate praise soon loses its effectiveness. To encourage an employee who already seems excessively self-confident may well make him conceited. Some individuals overreact to considerate treatment; they are the ones who, if you give them an inch, will take a yard. However, before passing judgment on such employees, the foreman should try to discover why they act as they do. Are they covering up a feeling of inferiority by a cocksure, superior manner, or do they really overestimate their ability? If the latter is the case, they will need to be shown their shortcomings in a tactful way. Sometimes, too, previous treatment by others has caused a person to develop a protective shell that can be misleading. To attempt to make such a person admit his inferiority will make him even more defensive.

In the long run, building employee self-esteem will produce far better results than will making employees feel inferior. Making an employee feel inferior may give a supervisor a temporary feeling of importance, but building his self-esteem will give both the employee and himself lasting satisfaction. Furthermore, it is far

Exhibit 6

Do's and Don'ts in Building Employee Self-Esteem

DON'TS	DO'S
Treat an Employee as an Individual	
Ignore employee.	Notice employee.
Fail to speak to employee.	Encourage suggestions.
Ignore suggestions.	Keep appointments promptly.
Keep employee waiting.	
Treat impersonally.	Call employee by name.
Show no interest.	Draw out in conversation.
Break promises.	Keep all promises.
Give Deserved Recognition	
Fail to give credit when due.	Be prompt in giving credit.
Praise results only.	Recognize effort as well as achievment.
Blame unfairly.	Be cautious in placing blame.
Fail to see potentialities.	Encourage initiative and talent.
Fail to let employee know progress.	Let employee know how he is doing.
Avoid Belittling	
Assume the "boss" attitude.	Treat employee as co-worker, not inferior.
Boast of one's position.	Allow employee to express opinions.
Assume superior attitude.	Talk *with*, not *at*, employee.
Dictate.	Suggest.
Speak in a loud voice.	Speak in moderate tones.
Use fear as a weapon.	Avoid use of threats.
Appear too busy to listen.	Take time to listen attentively.
Criticize thoughtlessly.	Criticize tactfully.
Criticize in public.	Criticize in private.
Criticize personally.	Be objective and impersonal.
Criticize only negatively.	Criticize constructively.
Nag.	Allow employee to correct own mistakes.
Withhold criticism when needed.	Give criticism when needed.
Anticipate failure.	Make employee feel he will succeed.
Use sarcasm or ridicule.	Avoid playing up oneself at employee's expense.

easier to lower morale than it is to build it up once it has been destroyed.

McGregor's Findings

In his book *The Human Side of Enterprise*[2] the late Douglas McGregor claimed that management has imposed severe limitations upon itself in the field of motivation by basing many of its decisions upon outmoded assumptions about human behavior.

The first of these assumptions—called "Theory X," is that most people have an inherent tendency to avoid work. The emphasis which management has placed on incentive pay and other rewards for performance, the evils of featherbedding (for railroad workers, musicians, and so on), and other limitations of output all reflect management's faith in this assumption.

The implementation of the first assumption leads to the second: that people must be coerced, controlled, and directed and that even such treatment is not enough to overcome their dislike for work. Management must even resort to threats of punishment in some cases.

These two assumptions and their consequences have led management to conclude that the average person does not want responsibility, has little ambition, and wants security above everything else and nothing beyond it. Therefore, management can only resort to the "carrot and stick" theory.

In contradiction to these old assumptions, McGregor sets forth a new set of assumptions, "Theory Y," which states that work is a very natural activity for most people and can be a source of satisfaction under the proper conditions. He further believes that the "carrot" will work only until a satisfactory subsistence and security level has been reached and that a person will go beyond that level when he is committed to objectives which he understands and which offer rewards of self-respect, the respect of associates, and the satisfaction of self-realization needs.

McGregor and Maslow are not far apart in their theories. They both are saying that all men have goals to be met or needs to be satisfied which lie beyond those of basic security and which man-

---

[2] McGraw-Hill Book Company, New York, 1960.

agement cannot satisfy. Only the individual can provide himself with self-respect, the respect of his fellows, and self-fulfillment.

Implications for Motivation

If the Maslow and McGregor theories are acceptable, the popular concept of the "motivator" must change. For many years, it was felt that a large part of a foreman's job consisted of motivating his people to do more and better work. It appears now that no foreman can motivate his people. His job is to create a climate or atmosphere in which people will motivate *themselves* to work at more nearly their full potential.

In generating the climate for self-motivation, the first step is to remove roadblocks from the path of greater productivity. The foreman must be willing, and be permitted, to let his people bite off as much as they can chew—and he must give them the freedom to make a mistake occasionally without paying too high a price.

So far this chapter has dealt with the basic human needs of every worker; however, every company has its own particular set of needs and the overall objective of survival. Competition must be met; and the company must operate at a profit, keep its costs down, and increase the volume of its business if it is to endure and grow in the free enterprise system. The foreman must make the company needs his own if he is to do the best possible job of leadership.

The key to motivation, then, is for the foreman to try to spell out for his subordinates the areas of common interest between their individual needs and the needs of the company. The more the two sets of needs can be made to coincide, the better motivated the workforce will be. Conversely, the greater the area of conflict between the company's and the employees' needs, the poorer the results will be.

Goal Setting

With the roadblocks removed, the foreman can begin to give his people something to shoot at; in other words, he can apply the goal-setting technique to them either as individuals or as a group.

The first step in the goal-setting process is to make the company goals known to the employees in terms that they understand. The foreman must keep in mind that company profit is not a goal—either for the company or for any individual in it. But profit may be an incentive and a yardstick of achievement that tells employees how well the company, through their efforts, has met the objectives. Thus the individual's pay check, profit-sharing bonus, or salary increase is a standard by which he can measure how well he is meeting the company goals.

The only goals that the foreman should be concerned with for his workers are those over which they have control. It may be that the company would like to reduce its scrap by 10 percent in a year; for the foreman this could mean a department goal of a 1 percent reduction each month. It may be a reduction of absenteeism, or it may be increased productivity through improved methods. There are many such possibilities, and more than one goal may be set.

Most important, the goals must represent a community of interest for the group, and they must be attainable. Goals that are too low offer neither challenge nor excitement; on the other hand, goals that are too high will discourage effort. Attaining a goal may be important, but it is not *all* important. Missing a target occasionally is not bad in itself. The important point is that the foreman find out why it was missed and make the corrections that will enable the group to hit it the next time.

These are a few ground rules for successful goal setting:

1. Let the employees submit their idea of an attainable goal to the foreman.
2. Have the foreman accept this goal or suggest an upward or downward revision.
3. Keep the goal above the present level.
4. Keep the goal within the range of the department's ability to operate successfully.
5. Make the goal specific. (Not, "Let's do better," but, "Let's set a goal of 10 percent over last month.")
6. Set up check points along the way and let people know how they are doing.

Above all, when goals are met, exceeded, or even almost met, the foreman should commend the group for its attainment or at least the effort put forth. He should be specific, pointing out why he likes the results and how the results benefit the group and the company. The feeling of being a part of a winning team is important because it satisfies the employee's need for self-esteem through recognition and identification as well as the company's need for a sound, well-working organization.

5

PERFORMANCE EVALUATION

IN PROFESSIONAL SPORTS, careful records are kept of the performance of each player. In baseball, batting, fielding, pitching, base-running, and base-stealing averages record the individual player's performance in terms of the specific factors that are important to the sport. This insures that the evaluation of players will be based on facts instead of impressions and opinions.

The same basic method should hold for industrial and commercial employees. Fair practice demands that men be rated on performance in terms of definite factors and not personal likes, dislikes, or snap judgments. Only an objective judgment of performance should determine whether Bill Jones or Joe Brown is of more value to the organization, has earned promotion, or merits an increase in pay.

Rating, judging, and evaluating are not new tasks devised by staff people to make more paperwork for foremen who are already busy. To some degree, every working person rates his fellow workers. He likes this boss better than that one; this clerk is more pleasant than the next; one foreman is more cooperative than another. And people continue making judgments in all aspects of their daily lives, not just at work. It is when a person becomes responsible for the work of others as a foreman that this evaluation process becomes significant. In fact, the foreman's ability to evaluate those under him may determine his success in his own job. He can't escape these facts any more than he can escape any other responsibility of foremanship.

Evaluation of performance is necessary—

1. To help in deciding who should be promoted or given a raise in pay.
2. To discover a worker's weaknesses as a basis for planning training.
3. To uncover exceptional talents.
4. To furnish a basis for discharge of a totally unfit employee.
5. To help top management learn how each employee is appraised by his foreman.
6. To help assign work in accordance with the worker's ability.
7. To serve as a check on employment procedures and tests.
8. To stimulate people to improve.
9. To develop employee morale through stimulating confidence in management's fairness.

There is no one best method of evaluation. Sometimes carefully devised systems are used; in other cases, no special system is developed, and the rating is done informally. In no case does the foreman have to wait until his company (through its staff people or with the help of outside consultants) develops a system for all to use. Since he continually evaluates his people, there is no reason why he cannot devise his own evaluation system for use within his own department.

The new legislation designed to insure equal employment opportunity regardless of race, creed, color, national origin, or age, should be a further indication to the foreman that his acts are subject to ever-closer scrutiny and review—with complaints following if he is considered to act in a prejudicial manner. Recognizing the delicacy of the related problems, the growing governmental pressures, and the moral implications, the foreman may have to challenge his own attitudes. The arguments for objective worker evaluation have never been stronger.

Rating Factors

Any system of rating a worker, whether simple or complex, is based upon six performance factors—the production factors of quantity of work and quality of work, the technical job knowledge factor, and the personality factors of adaptability, dependability, and cooperation. And there may be others as required. In a food processing plant, for example, cleanliness would be an important factor. In any case, as few performance factors as possible should be selected so as not to take too much of the foreman's time. Furthermore, the factors should be specifically defined to provide an accurate basis for consistent evaluation. Without precise definition, the foreman's interpretation of the factors might vary from time to time, and the result would inevitably be some degree of deviation from standard.

After the basic factors are determined, each factor should be divided into degrees. The three-grade scale of above average, average, and below average is the easiest to use and understand. The standards for each grade should be defined along with those for the basic factors.

The evaluation may utilize a point-value scale; that is, points are assigned to each performance factor to give a total of 100 for top performance and ability. The points will vary from factor to factor, depending upon the importance of each as related to the others and to the whole. For example, quantity of work might be given a point value of 20 for above average, 15 for average, and 10 for below average, whereas another factor might carry 15, 10, and 5 points for the same degrees. However, for all ordinary purposes and certainly for the foreman's personal use, a highly complicated point scale is not really necessary. The three-grade scale without numerical values is adequate for the usual purposes of rate adjustment, promotion, transfer, determination of training needs, layoff, dismissal, and so on.

The six basic performance factors cover the entire range of worker activity in most production situations. Note that "attitude" is not included. If a worker is above average or average in dependability and cooperation, he will have a positive attitude toward his organization. Attitude, in other words, is reflected in dependability and cooperation; it does not have to be listed separately.

Exhibit 7
Performance Chart

PERFORMANCE FACTOR *DEGREES OF FACTOR*

Quantity of Work	Above Average	Average	Below Average
Does the worker's production ability meet the demands of the job?	Production high. Unusually fast worker.	Production meets all normal requirements.	Production low. Slow worker.
Quality of Work			
Does he have the ability to meet quality standards?	High quality. Few rejects and errors. Does difficult jobs.	Work of good quality most of time. Some rejects and errors.	Careless. Many errors and rejects.
Job Knowledge			
Does he know his job?	Complete knowledge of job. Keeps up with new developments.	Knows the job fairly well, but could improve.	Does not know the whole job and is reluctant to learn.
Adaptability			
Does he adjust to changing conditions and learn new work?	Adjusts readily to change. Learns new work quickly.	Some resistance. Slowly adapts to new conditions and new work.	Resists change. Set in his work habits.
Cooperation			
Does he work well with others and willingly respond to an assignment even when it is inconvenient?	An excellent team worker. Ready response to difficult or unusual assignments.	Periodical friction with others. Some reluctance to do the difficult or unusual.	Difficulty with others. Does not want to inconvenience himself.

Exhibit 7 (*continued*)

Dependability	Above Average	Average	Below Average
Can he follow job instructions and complete his work assignments?	Does his job under any conditions to the best of his ability.	Will do the job correctly most of the time but some follow-up required.	Frequent follow-up needed on routine jobs.
Total Fitness			

Exhibit 7 is a completed evaluation chart using the six factors in three grades and eighteen degrees of performance.

How Often?

When should this necessary evaluation be done? Certainly, the new worker should be evaluated for the first time when the foreman is deciding whether to retain him. Of course, the man has just been evaluated as fit for the job, or he would not have been hired. However, most employees have a probationary period of 30 days or more. Most union contracts require a specific period of time to elapse before the union has control over the new employee, and the federal law specifies a minimum of 30 days. The first evaluation should be made just prior to the expiration of the probationary period.

Evaluation also helps during the new worker's training period. Proper, early judgment will make training easier by isolating the factors that make the employee satisfactory or unsatisfactory.

It is when a promotion is to be made, however, that worker evaluation assumes its greatest importance. Today more and more firms are interested in what the management experts call "executive development" programs, which involve promotion from within. Every supervisor is asked to recommend men in his department who have the potential to become good foremen. Unless the supervisor rates his men well, good candidates may be overlooked and poor candidates pushed into supervisory jobs for which they have no particular talents. Furthermore, more than one otherwise capable foreman has been passed over for promotion because he had no sucessor ready to step into his job.

Aside from probationary-period and prepromotion ratings, the foreman should evaluate all his employees systematically at least twice each year. It is better to rate the entire group at one time rather than to review each individual's performance on the anniversary of his date of hire. Comparisons have to be made which are best handled by evaluating the entire group. However, each employee should be evaluated on one factor before being evaluated on the next.

The "Halo Effect"

In all evaluations of other people, one difficulty stands out: It is unfair to make a total judgment of a person on the basis of liking or disliking one element in that person's character or personality. Dr. Harry Emerson Fosdick called this human tendency "thinking in bunches." For example, the young and pretty stenographer may be evaluated as "above average" by her boss even though she knows little about stenographic work. Personnel workers call this tendency "the halo effect."

It is this halo effect (or its opposite) that must be avoided by foremen who want to improve their judgment faculties. It is not an easy weakness to recognize and correct because it is all-pervasive, and, also, because it requires that a person recognize one of his own weaknesses—something that few people enjoy.

Some foremen like and expect a certain amount of "apple polishing." Employees quickly sense this, and some will readily comply. To such a foreman, a poor worker may wear a halo because he knows how to flatter his boss. And that boss will certainly make errors in his evaluation of his workers' abilities and potential because many good workers just will not do any "apple polishing."

Some foremen may be thrown out of balance by a beautiful face. For others, it may be equally difficult to judge objectively a man who is always complaining. Likewise, it may be very hard to make a proper evaluation of the young worker who is in line for the foreman's own job or of an employee who has ideas with which the foreman violently disagrees.

Every adult can think of similar examples from his own experience. The important step, however, is to recognize the danger of the halo effect in making sound evaluations. This recognition in itself will improve the foreman's judgment of those he supervises.

In any evaluation effort, there should be a few ground rules. For example:

1. Evaluate the worker's actual performance with a mind cleared of preconceived ideas.
2. Do not let unusual situations, personal feelings, or some recent incident influence the evaluation.
3. Concentrate on one factor at a time.
4. If a man's work is better than what one degree calls for, but not up to the next-higher degree, check the lower degree and add a plus sign.
5. Evaluate all employees at regular intervals (such as every six months). Evaluations between these specified times should be made for new employees or whenever some special decision is required.
6. After the evaluation has been made, check it against prior ratings to determine the worker's progress.
7. Review the evaluation with the worker in private.

The Rules Applied

The following cases are evaluated in terms of the chart shown as Exhibit 7:

Case 1—The drill press operator. Bill Jones is 32 years old and is a drill press operator, classified as a machine operator, for about five years. He has complained several times to his foreman of discrimination because he has never been made an assistant foreman. In his latest complaint, he stated emphatically that he was qualified for the job.

The foreman checks over Bill's qualifications and finds that the situation is about like this: Bill usually does a fairly good job, but there is nothing outstanding about his work. He is a good routine worker and knows his job fairly well, but he could never be classified as an expert. He gripes a little when he has to change jobs or shifts and learn new methods, but he eventually comes through.

He generally keeps busy and does not waste his time or take advantage of the foreman's absence, but the foreman has to check up on him occasionally to keep him in line. Bill usually gets along with his foreman and his fellow workers, but he occasionally gets quarrelsome and has to be pacified. He is not the first to agree to work overtime on his bowling night, but he can be persuaded.

In terms of the factors on the chart, Bill seems to rate about average in all areas, with a resulting average for total fitness. Obviously, he has no outstanding qualifications that indicate leadership ability. Since Bill's complaint is that he was being discriminated against in making selections for the job of assistant foreman, his supervisor should review this evaluation with him, pointing out the qualifications needed for promotion and how Bill may develop them through training.

Case 2—The molder operator. Jack Smith is a molder operator in a large bakery. He is 27 years old and has been working in the bakery production department for one and one-half years.

Under the union contract, a higher-grade job with a higher rate of pay has been posted for bidding. The union contract also provides that the open job is to be filled by the bidding worker who has the greatest seniority, provided that, in the judgment of management, he is qualified. Jack bids for the job along with two other employees who have less seniority.

The foreman's investigation reveals that Jack's work just about gets by; he is careless and has too many rejects—and this has been brought to his attention several times. He has never shown any desire to learn, his job knowledge is limited, and considerable time must be spent in teaching him new methods. He has considerable difficulty adjusting himself to new methods, new tools, and new conditions. The foreman and his assistants must keep an eye on Jack at all times, as he is inclined to disregard instructions and is frequently absent from his machine. He is continually involved in arguments with other workers and has very little interest in his job.

The foreman's evaluation indicates that Jack is below average in all factors except "adaptability," in which he is rated average. Because of this, the total fitness rating is below average with a plus. Jack is not deemed qualified to perform the higher-grade job.

Jack complains to his union, which, at first, comes to his defense. However, the shop committee members decide not to contest the grievance after they see the evaluation and the behavior upon which it is based.

Jack Smith was rated as better than average during his training and probationary period. It was after this that he slipped into below-average performance, which showed up in two prior evaluations. He should have been warned much earlier that he must improve or leave the company. Letting him continue at the substandard level can only mean to him and other workers that mediocre performance is acceptable to the foreman and the company.

Case 3—The mechanic. The maintenance foreman has a mechanic, Henry Johnson, whom he personally likes. Henry is about 35 and has been with the firm for about 8 years. There is a vacancy in the department for an assistant foreman, and the foreman decides to check Henry's qualifications carefully to see if he is eligible for promotion to this position.

Henry gets along very well with people and is always willing to carry more than his share of the load. He is deeply interested in his work and, when assigned a job, can be depended on to come through. However, he is a little slow in picking up new ideas; he has a tendency to continue with old and tried methods.

He is an unusually fast worker but, because of his speed, becomes a little careless at times. Usually, however, he does a good job. He knows his job better than the average worker, but he cannot be classified as an expert.

Henry Johnson's performance is rated as above average in quantity of work, dependability, and cooperation; average in adaptability; and average plus in quality of work and job knowledge. The total-fitness rating was average plus. If this mechanic can overcome the deficiencies shown in the evaluation and maintain the other elements of leadership which he seems to posses, he might make a good assistant foreman.

The foreman should summarize the results of each periodic evaluation of his entire workforce by listing the names and the total-fitness grades of each employee. Albert Walton, in his book *New Techniques for Supervisors and Men,* claims that the ratings should fall about as follow in the normal work group.*

---

* McGraw-Hill Book Company, New York, 1940.

Percent

Superior	2
Above average	14
Average	68
Below average	14
Subnormal	2

Under normal conditions, then, the foreman should find that approximately two-thirds of his group are evaluated as average. If the percentage is smaller than this, and there is a corresponding increase in the below-average group, it can only mean that either the evaluations have not been properly made or he has an unbalanced workforce.

When too few of his workers can make an average rating, the foreman must look into several factors:

1. His methods of evaluating his people.
2. His training methods, which may be insufficient or ineffective.
3. A hidden grievance that may be lowering worker morale.
4. Hiring procedures, which may have degenerated in a tight labor market.

In summary, knowledge and practice of the philosophy and techniques of performance evaluation greatly assist the foreman in doing a better job of directing the efforts of his subordinates.

6

DISCIPLINE PROBLEMS

THE WORD "discipline" comes from the Latin *disciplina,* which means "instruction." The dictionary definitions stress instruction rather than punishment or chastisement, giving "discipline" a very positive connotation, not nearly as negative as some people, including many foremen, seem to feel. It is not unusual to hear foremen ask, "What do I do to discipline this person?" when they actually mean that they don't know quite how to punish him. In the same way, parents are prone to say about children other than their own, "That child needs more discipline." If they mean that the child is in need of more instruction, they are probably right; if they mean that the child needs to be chastised more, they are not so likely to be right.

The Need for Rules

For the foreman, discipline is a practical day-to-day activity. Most employees would rather be a part of a well-trained, productive department headed by a good foreman where rules exist, are known, and are highly regarded, and in which standards are high enough to provide an incentive to achievement. People, in general, like the challenge of positive discipline; they want to know what is expected of them, and they respect a leader who requires that they meet expectations. They are more likely to do better work under such conditions than in a loosely managed group or department.

It necessarily follows that there must be established rules and regulations to be used as standards of behavior and performance by the workers. Individuals respond differently to the same situation; however, because society in general and business organizations in particular are made up of groups of people with common objectives, some degree of regulation must prevail for the good of the whole. True, there are still some companies (usually small ones) whose managers state that they have felt no need for rules thus far or that they prefer to take care of each situation as it comes along. This is neither sound thinking nor good management. These companies probably *have* a few rules, but they do not want to publicize them nor do they want to enforce them uniformly. Also, those rules which do exist may not be good ones. In cases of this kind (which, fortunately, are relatively few), the foreman is left to his own devices and must formulate his own departmental rules and regulations.

Where a union represents a group of employees and a labor-management agreement is in force, and where there are few if any stated company rules, the union will frequently get these rules into the contract. This is unwise because all contractual provisions become bargainable matters, whereas the establishment of company, plant, or department operating rules should remain a management right. The fact that rules find their way into union contracts is a clear indication that people want rules and that there can be no vacuum in this area. The rules in union contracts, however, are designed to benefit the employees and have little regard for the good of the company. Their presence also indicates that management has abdicated its responsibilities in part and allowed the union to take over a portion of its managerial duties.

No set of rules can be made to take care of every possible deviation from good conduct and performance. The unpredictability of human beings is just too great. But this should not be advanced as a reason for having no rules. Certainly a management can use its experience, including the records of disciplinary action in the past, as a basis for establishing regulations which will protect both company and employees against human weaknesses which will impede orderliness, health, and efficiency.

Some people constantly test the limits of acceptable behavior and satisfactory performance. (In *The Cost-Minded Manager,* John D. Staley states this as Staley's Fourth Law.[1]) For example, some automobile drivers test the tolerance of the state highway police, so that in some states five miles per hour over the limit has become an acceptable speed. Again, some new employees test the foreman's minimal requirements as to attendance, punctuality, or performance in general. Here is a typical conversation between a young female office worker and a business man, each unknown to the other, overheard recently in the elevator of a New York office building:

GIRL: Sir, do you have the time?

MAN (looking at his watch): It is now ten minutes to one.

GIRL: Gosh, I'm late again. This happens every day.

MAN: What time are you supposed to be back from lunch?

GIRL: Twelve forty-five.

MAN: What does your boss say about it?

GIRL: Nothing. I've worked here eight months, and if he hasn't said anything before he probably won't start now.

It is evident that the young lady in this case has tested the limits of her stated lunch "hour" and has stretched it by five minutes. The new starting time will probably be adopted by her whole group. If there are 24 girls in the group, this could mean a loss of two girl-hours per workday. And not only a loss of time is involved, for it is evident from the tone of the young lady's last statement that she has lost at least a small portion of her respect for the boss because he has not held her accountable to a standard or a rule of performance.

Making the Rules Known

Rules, whether they originate with top management (with the foreman participating) or with the foreman himself, should not be made just for the sake of making rules—or to keep in style. Rules should serve a known need, and the fewer the rules the better. To

---

[1] American Management Association, New York, 1961.

begin with, there are certain basic prohibitions which should be spelled out: for example, drinking or reporting for work under the influence of alcohol, stealing, gambling, smoking in restricted areas. Additional rules, as needed, can be introduced gradually so as to gain acceptance of them by the workers. Obviously, there is no point to establishing rules without acquainting the employees with them, and herein lies one of the foreman's chief responsibilities.

Ignorance of statute law is no excuse for violation of the law. But this is only partly true when company rules are violated. Management may have neglected to provide adequate information and so may be partly or largely to blame for an offense. In fact, if a union should take to arbitration the case of an employee discharged for violation of a rule he did not know existed, and if the employee were to prove that he did not know of the rule, the arbitrator would probably decide that the employee should be reinstated with back pay, thereby giving him an opportunity to work under a rule which he now knows.

Since the foreman is the one who must see that his employees know and understand company rules, he should be a party to their formulation. He is the person closest to the employees, therefore, he is in the best position to know what the needs are—that is, the reasons for the rules. Thus he is often able to suggest the wording which will make the rules most acceptable to his people. But not all rules, of course, will be companywide. A foreman may require a few regulations specifically applicable to his own department.

The following list covers the most frequent offenses for which rules and regulations are developed:

- Failure to report for work without good reason.
- Drunkenness or possession of liquor on the job.
- Willful damage to or removal of company property.
- Dishonesty, deception, fraud.
- Soliciting, canvassing, or circulating petitions on the job without permission.
- Falsifying records.
- Habitual tardiness without cause.
- Smoking in prohibited areas.
- Absence from department without permission.
- Abusive or threatening language.

- Fighting.
- Violation of known safety rules.
- Engaging in horseplay or practical jokes.
- Insubordination.
- Personal work done on company time without express permission.
- Failure to carry out reasonable orders.
- Absence beyond the approved number of days of leave or absence without notice.
- Gambling or conducting lotteries on company premises.
- Failure to punch own time card or punching another's time card.
- Concealing defective work.
- Preparing to leave the plant before quitting time.

This list is simply intended to be representative and is by no means complete. Almost every plant or department has particular problems, not covered here, for which rules must be drawn up.

Companies make their rules known to employees in a variety of ways. The most commonly used media are the following.

Employee handbooks. Recent surveys reveal that the employee handbook is considered a valuable device for circulating information about company rules and regulations. Usually a handbook of this kind contains more than the rules. It very often touches on the corrective measures to be used; thus it may state, for example, that violations of plant regulations will be sufficient grounds for disciplinary action and then proceed to spell out steps varying from reprimands and warnings to immediate discharge. Listing such corrective measures can be hazardous, and the wording should be thought out very carefully lest it make the stated steps mandatory and allow the foreman no latitude to use his own judgment.

Handbooks often include the course which the employee may pursue if he feels that he has been the victim of unfair or incomplete treatment in the enforcement of a rule or in the disciplinary action which follows any infraction.

Bulletin boards. Bulletin boards are widely used for posting regulations in plants where no employee handbook exists. Where a handbook is in use, the bulletin board still plays an important role in publicizing those rules which need particular emphasis, have been rescinded or changed, or have been made too recently to be included in the handbook.

Oral explanation. Oral explanation of rules by the foreman, personnel department staff, or others is almost a must. While such explanation sometimes merely supplements the handbook or material posted on the bulletin boards, it can serve to clarify doubtful points, soften the tone of a rule which, in cold print, may appear harsh, and provide an opportunity for the employee to ask questions and to express himself.

Miscellaneous methods. There are other media for the dissemination of rules and regulations to employees which are less frequently used but should also be considered. The union contract should, of course, be made known to all employees covered by it, whether it includes company rules or not. Practically all union contracts provide for seniority, grievance procedure, vacations, and so on, which are company policies rather than rules. Nevertheless, these should be clearly understood by the employees. Company or plant house organs or newspapers, payroll inserts, bulletins addressed to each employee, announcements over the company public address system, and orientation sessions all are proven communications devices.

Most companies do not limit themselves to just one of these media, nor do they substitute one for another. Dissemination of information about rules is so important that companies usually use some effective combination of media.

The new employee should be given copies of any printed matter available as well as an oral explanation (either individually or in a group). If the rules and regulations are extensive, he should be given the necessary facts in units which he can assimilate. A good follow-up system is essential during the probationary period. A new worker cannot be expected to learn all there is to know about the job and the company rules during the first day or even the first week at work.

 ## Rule Enforcement

After all the preliminary steps have been taken, it is necessary that the rules be enforced. This is the job of the man directly in charge: the foreman. Whenever rash behavior or violation of company rules on the part of an employee calls for disciplinary action, he finds himself in a very difficult decision-making area.

Improper discipline can be a costly venture. The "soft" foreman who prefers to overlook excesses is doing both his company and his employees a serious disservice. If, for example, he does nothing more than look the other way when a "wise guy" indulges in horseplay, he will surely regret his laxness should a serious injury later result when a second employee decides to have some "fun."

The foreman, in short, must be concerned about the handling of disciplinary problems, but he should not let this concern cause him to lose confidence in himself as a foreman. In fact, he has more reason to worry about his foremanship if he is *not* concerned about employee discipline. Just as is true in many other situations, those foremen who do not think much about disciplinary matters are usually the ones who *should be* most concerned.

Discipline, as stated at the beginning of this chapter, should have as its intent the correction of wrong thinking. It is a form of teaching, not punishment. When discipline is used for punishment alone, the usual result is greater and more intense antagonism on the part of the individual being disciplined. Nobody likes to be criticized—particularly when the criticism is in no way constructive.

For example, in the baking industry, production employees work on Sunday and are off on Saturday. However, Sunday is a day of religious significance for many people, and on Sunday absenteeism in some shops is higher than on any other day of the week. Moreover, since Sunday is usually a high production day, absenteeism on Sunday imposes a greater hardship on the supervisor and other employees. Often a foreman will punish a Sunday absentee by giving him one or more additional days off without pay—an action that seems self-contradictory. The foreman does not like or want absenteeism (especially on Sunday) because the efforts of all employees are needed, yet he proceeds to deny that need by *demanding* that a particular employee be absent for one or more additional days.

This is an example of what can only be called thoughtless discipline—discipline motivated by emotions rather than by wisdom. It cannot be considered conducive to the correction of wrong thinking for the foreman to create more absenteeism for the employee and himself.

If an employee makes a mistake out of carelessness, any disciplinary action that may be taken is merely punitive. The cause of the careless act must be determined before the foreman can couple punitive action (if any) with corrective action. To be sure, not all actions by employees can be corrected, but in virtually all cases the attempt can be made. Certainly, when an employee who has a good record suddenly makes an error or breaks a rule, the cause should be carefully determined. The employee's behavior may be a direct reflection on the foreman's ability. The poorest and most self-damaging explanation a foreman can offer his superior about something that has gone wrong is "Bill was careless" or "None of my people cooperate." Statements of this kind call for considerable self-examination.

For example, take the employee who has had a good record during his employment of more than a year but who suddenly becomes careless and sloppy in his work. His rejects are so high that the foreman feels disciplinary action is needed. Before taking action, the foreman tries to discover the reason for this sudden letdown; and in looking over the records, the foreman finds that the employee started to go downhill about two weeks before, just at the time when a general pay increase went into effect. Further investigation reveals that this particular employee's pay had *not* been raised—through an error in the payroll department which was immediately corrected. But, as a result of the error, the employee now feels that if "they" don't care any more than they seem to, why should he?

Naturally, the foreman had the oversight corrected the minute it came to his attention, and the employee may again become a useful, productive worker. Nevertheless, some damage has been done. The employee—illogically perhaps—cannot help but suspect that an attempt was made to discriminate against him. To the extent that the foreman did not anticipate this very natural feeling, he was to blame. At least he did not discipline the faltering employee without investigating the cause of the trouble. That would have been grossly unfair; and both the employee and the company, including the foreman, would have been the losers.

If there is any general rule to be drawn from such cases it is that *the foreman should use discipline with care—and only after he is sure that he has all the facts.*

There are very few rule violations which warrant summary discharge. Possibly proven theft is one, but even for so serious an offense the employee is often simply suspended without pay, pending the outcome of a full investigation. Most other infractions require at least one warning before any penalty, including discharge, is imposed. Discharge is an extreme form of punishment and should be resorted to only after the foreman has made several attempts to correct the employee and has warned him about what will happen if the violation continues for a specific period of time or if it happens again within a specified period of time. (See Chapter 10.)

Every counseling session should be written up, and the resulting memo should be placed in the employee's file. This is especially true of any warnings. And, where a union is involved, it is best to send a copy of the warning to the union with notes of the prior attempts at correction. If the union stewards have any fault to find with the handling of the case, they will probably voice their feelings immediately. If they do not, they will probably not contest the case at a later date if discharge takes place. Many times a union business agent or steward will tell the employee that the company acted within its rights and, if the employee is discharged, the union will not defend him. Frequently, he mends his ways when he learns that he no longer has the support and protection of his union.

There should be a limit to the time during which a warning is carried in the file. No man should live in a state of irredeemable sin. If the warning states that the next time thus and so happens, the employee will be discharged, and if the employee corrects the situation and works well for several years, he should not be discharged after so long a period for another offense of the same kind. The time limit should of course vary with the gravity of the case and the past history of the employee. Time limits on warnings are very much like the limits on a suspended sentence in court and the statute of limitations in law.

Self-Discipline Is the Best

It is often effective to point out to an erring employee that a person cannot withdraw money from a bank unless he has put money in and, by the same token, cannot borrow money if his credit is poor.

In a working situation, there is always a time when the employee will ask some small concession from his foreman. He may want to get off an hour early to meet his son, who is returning home after a year in a foreign country in the army. Or he may want to get an early start on a vacation trip. Each request, in itself, is a rather small matter. The foreman will usually want to grant the favor or even volunteer to give the employee a break. However, no matter how much he would like to do it, the foreman cannot if his hands are tied—and the employee frequently and unwittingly ties them by having nothing in the bank when he wants to make a withdrawal. If this situation is pointed out to the employee when tardiness appears to be on the increase or when he is absent more and more for flimsy reasons, the foreman will often not have to take unpleasant disciplinary action. The employee will discipline himself, and that is the best form of discipline, especially with an entire group in which each man polices himself.

The foreman cannot expect self-discipline from his employees if he does not have it himself. Here again he sets the example. Self-discipline for the foreman does not mean that he punishes himself or makes a martyr of himself: It is reflected in his planning and organization of his job. He knows *what* he wants done and *how* it should be done. He takes the blame when it is his fault. He is not guilty of lost motions or indecision. He knows that the best leadership is constant and consistent. Standards of performance do not change to suit his convenience or that of a favorite employee. He asks more of himself than of his employees and thus gets all he asks from them.

Typical Decisions

A few actual cases will help to illustrate these points. The following cases arose within the Ford Motor Company, and the decisions are those of Harry Shulman, impartial umpire at the time.[2] Employee names are fictitious.

Case 1. Art Conroy, an employee with five years' seniority, was penalized five times for absenteeism and discharged for his sixth

[2] Laurence Stessin, "Right and Wrong in Employee Discipline, *Industrial Management Symposium,* Consolidated Printing Company, 1953.

violation. Conroy attempted to justify his absence by citing illness in his family and damage to his household furnishings by fire. The umpire decided that since Art had previously been put on probation three times and continued to be absent even during his periods of probation, his absenteeism was "chronic and excessive without adequate justification." *The discharge was sustained.*

Case 2. Ben Wade was discharged for striking a fellow employee on the head with a hammer. Wade claimed provocation in that the other employee called him a name reflecting upon his color and ancestry. In the words of the umpire, however, "No verbal provocation justifies such an assault under the law of the land or the law of the shop." *The discharge was sustained.*

Case 3. Pete Burke was found smoking during an unexcused absence from his job. He was also charged with a number of other offenses relating to incidents long past, of which no record had been kept and for which no penalties had been imposed. Burke was discharged on constant and habitual breach of company rules. The umpire stated: "Past breach of company rules is not of itself a ground for disciplining an employee at some later time. His past conduct is merely a matter to be taken into account in determining the penalty to be imposed for a current breach." *Burke was reinstated with back pay.*

Case 4. Joe Crane, an employee for seven months, was fired because he worked too slowly on the job. He had been shifted from foreman to foreman to see whether he could produce adequately under different men. He had worked for at least four foremen in his seven months of employment, and each of them complained of his inadequate production. The union claimed that the six months' probationary period provided sufficient time in which to discover whether an employee was qualified and, since Crane had completed this probationary period, he should not be discharged. The umpire disagreed as follows:

> True, the company could have made its determination earlier and during the probationary period. But the fact that the company did not discharge him earlier does not give him a vested right to inadequate production. And the fact that he passed his probationary period does not give him unimpeachable life tenure. Crane was discharged for proper cause and his grievance must be denied.

The discharge was upheld.

Case 5. Tom Kelly, in performing his job, used a hammer and a screwdriver to force aluminum tubes together through bolted brackets, thus damaging the tubes in a way that could have had catastrophic results for a bomber in flight. He was discharged for gross negligence, but Kelly claimed he had never been told how to perform the job. The umpire upheld his claim:

> Kelly had never been instructed otherwise and had never been warned about the hazard either by supervision or by any fellow employee. Though the harmful consequences of his action were great and could have been disastrous, his own fault was nowhere near as great. He was doing his work honestly and faithfully and erred only because of a lack of instructions or experience or judgment, and because of the way he had been broken in on the job.

Kelly was reinstated.

Case 6. Jack Martin was given a two-day disciplinary layoff for distributing campaign literature in support of his candidacy for union office. The umpire's decision was as follows:

> Martin seems to assume that so long as he was using his own time, he was entitled to engage in this activity on company property. He overlooks the fact that he was using company property for his activity and subjecting it to the possible consequences of the distribution of literature in a busy aisle. The contract prohibits "soliciting on company property without permission." There was no permission here.

The penalty was sustained.

To help make certain that disciplinary action will stick, the following basic ground rules should be kept in mind:

1. Policies, rules, and standards must be stated clearly. Don't expect anything not clearly written and stated to be "understood." If the foreman wants the employee himself to notify him in the event of absence, the rules should state so. If the rules simply provide that notice shall be given, the employee may tell someone else to call the foreman or give the message to another employee, thereby shifting the responsibility.

2. Policies and rules should be made known to all employees. Rules should be posted. Each employee should be given a copy of a manual or handbook. New employees should be briefed about the rules as part of their orientation.
3. Every incident of nonadherence to rules must be recorded by the foreman (time, place, and essential facts).
4. The individual should be interviewed when he breaks a rule or his performance is substandard. After he has been given an opportunity to explain, the matter can be reviewed and the decision made known to him in a straightforward manner. The absence of "positive evidence" to support charges has blocked many attempts to discipline an offender, no matter how just the complaint.
5. If a warning is issued, it should be submitted in writing and, preferably, be signed by the employee.
6. If the warning includes notification of more severe action for the next infraction, this should be clear and unqualified.
7. Personnel files should be maintained for each employee, so that the offender's background and record are available, as well as those of other employees in his department or classification.
8. Five major factors should be considered in determining a penalty. Any one factor or combination of factors could serve to mitigate the offense and make the maximum penalty inadvisable:
   ▪ Provocation, if any, for the violation.
   ▪ Nature of the rule or regulation violated.
   ▪ Gravity of the consequences of violating the rule.
   ▪ Prior record of the offender.
   ▪ Length of time the offender has been employed by the company.
9. The breach of a rule should be clear-cut before a penalty is imposed.

7

ADJUSTMENT OF GRIEVANCES

ADJUSTING WORKERS' GRIEVANCES is one of the most important of modern management techniques. It is particularly important to the first-line supervisor or foreman. Not only are most grievances directed to him for attention, but most should be adjusted by him.

And prompt grievance adjustment is as important as satisfactory grievance adjustment if good employee morale is to be maintained, much less improved. If grievances are not heard at all or, if heard, not attended to promptly and satisfactorily, low worker morale may develop into serious labor trouble, expensive to both workers and management.

Because of our relatively limited knowledge of the complex human personality, the adjustment of grievances cannot be classified as an exact science. However, through trial and error plus some research and experiment, effective methods for the adjustment have been developed.

When a new piece of equipment is brought into the office or the plant, the supervisor or foreman will read the specifications and the operating manual and study the machine itself. He does all this diligently in order that he may understand the way in which the machine functions, the number and type of operations that can be performed on it, and its capacity. He recognizes that a major portion of his responsibility consists in knowing "machine behavior." And because he has this knowledge, and consequently can predict what will happen to that piece of equipment when the principles of mechanics, physics, or electronics are violated, he does not violate these principles, nor does he permit his employees to violate them.

And it is so with people, although the employee is much more complex than any machine. He has feelings, he is motivated by many forces, and he has the ability to adjust to many climates. Nevertheless, his behavior can be understood and, in many situations predicted, if a few basic motivational factors are considered. Thus a supervisor should be able to predict that a grievance will develop in a person when certain principles of human behavior have been violated.

What Is a Grievance?

Most American workers are good, law-abiding citizens who want to go their way peacefully in an untroubled atmosphere. Occasionally one may take aggressive action to get what he maintains are his rights. In business, an employee takes "aggressive action" when he seeks an adjustment to a grievance.

The Oxford Universal Dictionary defines a grievance as follows: "a circumstance or state of things felt to be oppressive. In modern use, something (real or supposed) which is considered a legitimate ground of complaint." The same dictionary defines a complaint as an "utterance of grievance; a statement of injustice suffered." A grievance, then, is a "state of things," and a complaint is the expression of this state. A person may have a grievance without ever putting it into words; a supervisor may have several grievances within his group of employees and actually hear about none of them.

The Development of Grievances

Usually the employee's reaction to a grievance is one of annoyance, distress, or some form of resentment. His emotions usually follow this pattern:

FRUSTRATION——→RESENTMENT——→AGGRESSION

For example, if a child wants an ice cream cone which his parents deny him for any reason, he will be frustrated, resentment will develop, and his aggressive action may take the form of sulking or crying. Depending upon the child's age and cleverness he may even react by breaking open his bank to obtain the price of the ice cream cone or doing some work to earn the money to buy the cone.

In any case, the frustrated child will be resentful and take aggressive action in some form sooner or later. No one taught him to react this way; it is part of his psychological make-up. The same cycle applies to all human beings.

Here is an example of how the frustration cycle works in an adult. A worker asked his foreman one Friday afternoon if he could advance his vacation date and leave the following Friday for his week's vacation. Three friends of his had arranged a fishing trip and had invited him along as the fourth. The foreman said he would check the workload to see if the employee could be spared.

On Monday afternoon, the employee again approached the foreman and asked if the change of vacation date was possible. The foreman said he thought it might be arranged, thus giving the worker the impression that permission had been given to leave on Friday.

On Thursday afternoon, the foreman told the worker that he had checked the workload, and the worker could not be spared. He would thus have to take his vacation as originally scheduled. The worker protested, stating that he had made all his arrangements Monday night after the foreman had "approved" the change in date. It was too late now for his friends to get a new fourth, and as they were counting on his sharing the expense of the trip, backing out now would be difficult and embarrassing for him.

The foreman stated emphatically that he had only said he thought the change of vacation *might* be arranged; he had not given final approval. The worker angrily protested. The foreman refused to reconsider, and the worker did not go on his fishing trip.

This incident is a good example of how a grievance can develop. A desired course of action was frustrated; and, of course, the worker was annoyed or distressed, not only because he could not go fishing when he wanted but also because he could not keep his promise of sharing expenses with his friends and was "in bad" with them.

Grievances, then, are caused by the frustrations which develop when actual or desired courses of action have been prevented expression. Even if the frustrations are only related to or indirectly connected with the job, they *must* be neutralized in order to adjust the grievance.

Grievance Areas

It is now generally accepted that virtually all grievances originate in one, two, or all three of the following areas:

1. *Conditions outside the job.* These may be related to family conditions, social life, labor conditions in the area, religious obligations, or other phases of the worker's life. In general, he has an off-the-job problem which has caused him to be dissatisfied with his job, and he is looking for an on-the-job adjustment to solve the problem.
2. *Conditions on the job.* These are directly related to happenings on the job. Whether actual, imagined, or based on misunderstanding, they frequently involve working conditions in the department or plant, the immediate supervisor, the application of company policies or the absence of them, working hours, or wages. Many of these job conditions cause dissatisfaction in more than one employee and give rise to group action.
3. *Conditions within the employee.* These are a reflection of the individual's temperament, background, personal convictions and attitudes, and physical condition. They are of course subjective in nature; yet, when they give rise to problems, the worker may seek an objective adjustment on the job.

A few examples may help to clarify the three areas of grievances. (See Exhibit 8.) For instance, an employee will occasionally complain to his supervisor that he is not getting as much overtime as the others in the group even though the time records over a period of time show that he has an equal share of the overtime. The supervisor may also learn that the employee is in debt and needs money because of his extravagant standard of living. This is a condition outside the job which is causing the employee to be dissatisfied with

(*text continues on page 94*)

Exhibit 8

Areas of Grievances

I. OUTSIDE THE JOB

Family Conditions:
Attitude of wife
Extramarital affairs
Problem children
Relatives
Financial pressure
Extravagance
Sickness or death

Social Life:
Late hours
Too much entertaining
Too many off-the-job activities

Contemporary Trends:
Labor
Sports
Politics
War
Income tax

Environment:
Religious or racial obligations

Labor Conditions:
Transportation
Weather
Previous job
New industries
—Higher pay
—Better working conditions

General:
Living conditions
Rumors
Legal worries

Conclusion: Conditions outside the job can cause the employee to be dissatisfied with his job and develop a grievance. He hopes through a job adjustment to solve his off-the-job problem.

II. ON THE JOB

Working Conditions:
Unhealthful environment
Unsafe equipment or practices
Poor equipment
Old and obsolete methods
Poor housekeeping
Unreasonable time schedules
Inadequate lunch periods, lunchroom
Inadequate rest periods, rest room

Company Policies:
None—each foreman makes his own
Vacations indefinite
Health insurance pension plan, credit union missing or inadequate

Working Hours:
Irregularity
Night work

Exhibit 8 (*continued*)

Working Conditions (*con.*)
Inadequate washrooms, lockers, etc.
Unsatisfactory temperature, light, ventilation
Crowding
Poor chairs, benches

Foreman:
Not interested in his people
Shows favoritism
Has a closed mind
Cannot control his emotions
Violates worker's personality
Is a slavedriver
Makes promises not kept
Does not train properly
Does not upgrade
Keeps vacation schedule indefinite
Sets bad example

Working Hours (*con.*)
Short hours
Overtime
Split shift
Holidays

Plant Conditions:
Parking inadequate
Plant location inconvenient
Transportation poor
No protection in bad neighborhood

Wages:
Rates lower than area average
Too little or too much overtime
Bonus system not understood
Provisions for wage increases not clear

Conclusion: Unsatisfactory conditions on the job cause the employee to be discontented with his job and develop a grievance. Many of the on-the-job conditions affect the workers as a group, and so cause group grievances which may result in serious labor trouble.

III. WITHIN THE WORKER

Temperament:
Jealous
Grouchy
Complaining
Negative
Aggressive
Prejudiced
Suspicious
Disloyal
Thoughtless of others
Stubborn
Unreliable
Proud

Physical Conditions:
Habits
Dress
Cleanliness
Defects or deformities
Physique
Strength
Endurance
Height
Allergies
Sight
Hearing
General health conditions

Exhibit 8 (*continued*)

Background:
  Religion
  Race
  Political convictions
  Education
  Environment

Fixed Attitudes:
  Strong personal convictions
    about religion, politics, race,
    labor, management, war, and
    others

Complexes:
  Inferiority
  Superiority
  Fear

Conclusion: Conditions within the employee may cause him to be dissatisfied with his job and develop a grievance. He seeks through a job adjustment to solve the problem created within himself.

---

his job because it does not provide him with the income necessary to meet his debts.

Then, again, operators on an incentive bonus frequently develop grievances because faulty equipment impedes their productivity and reduces their pay. This is clearly an on-the-job condition which is easily corrected. The alert supervisor, the one who is interested in his employees, will keep the on-the-job frustrations to a minimum.

Finally, there is the case of the employee who was conscientious and efficient in his work because he was very ambitious. He wanted to be promoted to a supervisory position, since this would give him an income large enough to send his two children to college—an advantage which he had been denied. He had been told that he had the qualifications for promotion even though the company did not usually promote workers to supervisory positions.

However, when the supervisor's position was open, a new man was hired from outside the company. After being thwarted in this way, the ambitious worker turned his efforts to winning the office of president of his union. This took him five years. A bitter struggle between the union and management followed, and the company was forced to promote qualified men from the ranks to supervisory positions.

The area of this grievance encompasses all three sets of conditions. The grievance arose from outside the job because the employee wanted to earn more money to educate his children, and he was frustrated on the job because he wanted to be a supervisor in spite of the company's policy of hiring from the outside. And, finally, there was frustration within the employee (probably his strongest motivation) because he was intelligent and ambitious and wanted the gratification and prestige which go with promotion. He finally succeeded in this third area—but through his union.

It is essential that the true area of the grievance be determined by the foreman; for, unless it is found, no satisfactory adjustment can be made. Therefore, the foreman should not blindly accept the employee's explanation of his grievance. The worker may be concealing it or may not even know its true source. The supervisor should question the employee and check conditions in all three areas.

Types of Grievance

After the area of the grievance has been determined, the type of grievance must also be ascertained. For, as with areas, there are three *types* of grievance:
1. *Real grievance.* This is an actual situation on the job which frustrates the worker.
2. *Imaginary grievance.* This is a grievance which exists only in the worker's imagination. It may be based, however, on actual facts which have been misinterpreted, misunderstood, or distorted by the worker.
3. *Substitute grievance.* Either because he does not know or does not want to reveal the true cause of his grievance, the worker substitutes another cause for it.

Grievance Warnings

As was stated earlier, there is a vast difference between a grievance and a complaint. Furthermore, there are many ways in which a worker may take aggressive action besides expressing it in words. In addition, there is the possibility that the resentment phase of the frustration cycle may run on for a long period of time before the worker takes any discernible action.

During the interval prior to the open complaint or other clear aggressive action, the alert supervisor can detect the development of a grievance through changes in employee attitude and performance. These shifts in behavior are the grievance danger signals, and, if they are detected, the supervisor can take corrective action before the grievance becomes fullblown. The detection of incipient grievances is just as fundamental as the adjustment of actual grievances. It is to the supervisor's advantage to understand this and to act when the signals first become apparent. There are three basic types.

The first danger signal is when the ordinarily noncomplaining employee becomes a chronic complainer. His complaints are continual and concern such working conditions as heat, cold, ventilation, parking, schedules, and travel. These complaints are usually made to other workers and are general rather than specific.

Second, the worker may show evidence of losing interest in his job. He becomes less effective; that is, there is a drop in his productivity, he makes more errors than before, and he is involved in more accidents. Or he may be tardy, absent, or away from his workplace more than usual.

The third danger signal is a negative attitude. The worker becomes noncooperative, sulking, almost insubordinate, and generally antagonistic toward management. He is preoccupied and seems to be brooding over something.

When these danger signals appear alone or in combination, it is incumbent upon the foreman to take action to correct the situation. If he can do this, worker morale will be improved and he will have more time for the other important elements of his job.

The Adjustment Process

The first step in the solution of any problem is to determine and set down all the facts. This requires patience and methodical pursuit; the sooner it is begun, the better. The foreman should act without delay at the first indication of a danger signal.

The employee should be allowed to tell his story privately. In that way the foreman will be more likely to get the facts as the worker sees them, and the employee will be able to "get it off his chest." Often the mere recital of wrongs or alleged wrongs to a sympathetic listener will make the speaker feel less bitter.

The foreman, through questioning, can help the employee think more clearly about his grievance. Many times the employee is emotional. Questions tend to quiet him down so that facts not included in the original story may emerge. In many cases this questioning by the foreman will cause the employee to amend his story. The foreman then should repeat aloud the amended story, get the employee's agreement to it, or amend the story again. This is important: The employee's agreement must be secured.

If other employees are involved, the foreman should question them privately. He may also have to check time, production, and other records to get additional facts.

The second step is one of analyzing the data and arriving at a decision. This can be difficult, and it always takes time. Usually there is more than one possible adjustment of the grievance. Each should be listed on a sheet of paper. The foreman should then carefully analyze the possibilities and consider the effect of each adjustment on the employee, on other people who may be involved, directly or indirectly, and on production.

The foreman's analysis should indicate the one adjustment that will be fair and satisfactory to all persons and elements involved and will neutralize the employee's frustration by giving the employee what he wants, providing a satisfactory substitute, or changing his attitude.

All this frequently takes more time than the complaining employee feels is necessary. Therefore, it is extremely important that the supervisor keep the employee informed of his progress. In any case, the decision must be made before the supervisor is ready to take the third step, the actual adjustment. This should begin as quickly as possible after the complaint has been made and the danger signal or signals investigated.

At this point, it is important to determine exactly who has jurisdiction. Can the foreman make the decision, or does the grievance involve other departments, changes in company policy, or modifications of procedures? Perhaps the grievance may have to be referred to a higher authority. If so, the foreman should act accordingly—but reserve for himself the prerogative of conveying the decision to the employee.

The foreman should take the employee to his office or some other private place, put him at ease, and in a friendly way begin the adjustment of the grievance by private counseling. This involves deliberating with the employee and giving advice. Since the foreman should now understand all phases of the grievance, he should be in a position to discuss it intelligently and make constructive suggestions. His procedure should be to ask the worker well-planned questions and, in that way, encourage him to think through his problem.

When the area of the grievance is outside the job or within the worker or when the grievance is imaginary or the result of a misunderstanding, the primary adjustment to be made is in the worker's thinking and feeling about the grievance. The foreman cannot change the conditions in the employee's home life which may be the basis of a substitute grievance, but he can, by counseling with the worker, make him aware of the real source of his trouble. The employee can then try to change conditions at home or resign himself philosophically to the situation. The same thing holds true for an on-the-job grievance, although the foreman can often do more than advise in these cases. He cannot change the location of the factory, but he may be able to help the employee work out his transportation problem.

The worker must accept the adjustment of the grievance; otherwise the foreman's effort in his behalf has been futile. Getting the worker's acceptance does not mean out-arguing him or suppressing him with the weight of authority. Under these conditions he will *say* that he is satisfied, but he will go back to the job and complain to his associates or to the union steward that he has "been taken for a ride." To gain the worker's cooperation, his frustration must have been neutralized and his attitude shifted from negative to positive. His acceptance then will be spontaneous and permanent.

When the grievance adjustment has been made, one more step remains to be taken—follow-up. The foreman must assure himself that the adjustment has been satisfactory to the employee and to other employees involved and that the effect on production has been good. Follow-up should take place within a reasonable time after the employee has accepted the adjustment—not too soon and not too late; the situation should indicate the correct time lapse. Moreover, follow-up should be casual; the employee should not be aware of it. He should simply be observed in a quiet way and asked some questions about his job. His reactions should indicate whether his attitude is positive and if he is happy in his work environment.

The other employees involved also should be observed and questioned casually in order to get their reactions. Particular attention should be given to group morale.

In many cases, the foreman's primary concern in adjusting the grievance is its effect on production. Production figures for the individual and the entire department should be watched until the foreman is satisfied that there has been no adverse effect.

If, during follow-up, the foreman finds that for whatever reason the results are not good, he can only conclude that the grievance has not been satisfactorily adjusted. What should he do? He should readjust the grievance, starting with Step 1. He may not have found all the facts the first time, or he may not have analyzed the facts properly. Perhaps he did not handle the adjustment correctly; his counseling may not have been thorough, or he may have out-argued the worker and forced his acceptance.

The Four Steps Illustrated

Here is a grievance case which illustrates the proper adjustment procedure.

A bookkeeper in the general office, Bill Brown, asked the office manager for a transfer to the payroll department of the plant office on the other side of town. The office manager was surprised because, for five years, Bill had never voiced any dissatisfaction and was one of the best young men in the general office. The office manager told him that he didn't want to lose him and asked if there was anything wrong.

Bill responded by saying that he had grown tired of the monotony of the job. The office manager explained that the plant office job would pay less and require more travel to and from home. Bill stated that he knew and accepted this.

The office manager said he would consider Bill's request but was puzzled because Bill had never complained about the job before. He decided to investigate further before making the transfer. Three days later, Bill asked again about the transfer. "The noise is making me nervous," he said. The office manager suggested that Bill see a doctor at company expense, but Bill insisted that he didn't need a doctor and just wanted to get out of the general office immediately.

The office manager agreed to speak to the controller about the transfer, but he was still puzzled and felt quite certain that Bill was not giving the real reason for his request. Since Bill had never complained before about the monotony or the noise, there must, the office manager felt, be a deeper cause. He determined to find it by trying to recall every bit of information that he had about Bill.

Bill was 26 years old, intelligent, healthy—a fine worker and a wholesome person. He was saving money regularly to make a down payment on a home for himself and the girl whom he expected to marry in about a year. However, according to the grapevine, Bill's fiancee was now dating Joe Smith. Joe—a little younger than Bill and very good looking—worked in the same room with Bill. In fact, Bill had helped Joe get the job about two years ago and had been friendly with him ever since. How did Bill feel about Joe now? Could this be the real grievance?

The office manager took another day to check up on the rumors and found that they were correct. Bill's engagement had been broken, and Joe was now engaged to the girl. Joe had openly boasted of this. So Bill's thinking was now evident: If he were transferred to the plant office, he would not have to see Joe every day and relive his humiliation.

In reviewing the situation, the office manager recognized that Bill was an excellent bookkeeper and popular with his fellow workers. Joe was careless; and, if put in Bill's job, he would probably not make the grade. The manager had warned Joe about his work several times before, but Bill had asked him to give Joe another chance and had helped him do better each time. Bill was needed and would be difficult to replace.

What had the manager to do? He made the chart of the grievance that is presented in Exhibit 9.

Exhibit 9

Adjustment of a Grievance

STEP I—DETERMINE THE FACTS

Complaint

Bill Brown asked for a transfer to the payroll department in the plant office.

Bill was a good bookkeeper.

Bill complained about the monotony of the job; the office manager agreed to consider transfer.

Three days later Bill again asked for transfer. The noise was making him nervous, he said.

The office manager agreed to speak to the controller about Bill's request.

Additional Facts

Bill had never complained about the monotony or the noise before.

Bill was intelligent, a good worker, had been engaged to a girl who was now engaged to a co-worker, Joe Smith. Bill and Joe had been good friends. Bill apparently did not want to work in the same office with Joe any longer.

Joe was below average as a bookkeeper.

Bill was needed and difficult to replace.

Bill was popular in the office. Joe was not.

STEP II—ANALYZE AND DECIDE

Grievance area: Within the employee.
Possible adjustments:

1. Transfer Bill Brown as requested.

Grievance type: Substitute.

Bill might be satisfied, but only temporarily at best.

Frustration would not be neutralized, and he might develop a negative attitude. Other office employees might be resentful over the transfer. Productivity could drop.

2. Refuse transfer

Bill's frustration would grow deeper, and his productivity and interest would probably drop.

Exhibit 9 (*continued*)

3. Talk to Bill about the girl. Point out that a girl as fickle as she might have led him a difficult life had he married her.	Bill might resent the intrusion into his personal affairs.
4. Transfer Joe Smith. Speak to Bill and ask him to stay.	Joe is not good at his present job but might do better in the plant office. Bill would probably withdraw his request for transfer.

Final decision for adjustment: Transfer Joe. Tell Bill about the plan and ask him to stay temporarily.

STEP III—TAKE ACTION

Action taken by the office manager:
The transfer of Joe Smith was discussed with controller, who agreed with the plan. The office manager then talked with Joe privately, pointing to his past difficulties in the accounting department and to the possibility that Joe could do better financially in the plant office over the long run (a necessity for a man who was planning on being married). After some discussion, Joe agreed to the transfer.

The office manager next talked with Bill privately and told him why Joe was going to be transferred. Since this move would leave the general office accounting department short-handed, he asked Bill to stay until a replacement could be obtained.

Bill stated that he felt that his reasons for asking for the transfer were not really good; he would stay and forget about the transfer. He withdrew his request for a transfer.

STEP IV—FOLLOW-UP

Effect on Bill: Bill went back to his job as enthusiastic and satisfied as he had been in the past.

Effect on Joe: Joe seems to be contented. He learned the work quickly and is on the road to making more money.

Effect on other employees: Morale in the general office accounting department improved after Joe was transferred.

Effect on productivity: Bill's work in the general office accounting improved. Joe's output in the plant payroll department is about average.

If he intelligently considers all the factors involved, it is entirely possible for an employee to make his own adjustment to a grievance; he often does when he has a good foreman. Many employees realize that some situations are beyond the control of their supervisors and even of top management.

However, this self-adjustment requires a good foreman whose people respect and like him, who understands his employees, who listens to their problems, and who encourages them to bring these problems to him.

There is no grievance adjustment plan that every foreman can follow to a guaranteed solution; each case is different, each employee is different, and each foreman is different. The broad principles set forth in this chapter should, when sincerely applied, result in satisfactory adjustments in about 85 percent of all cases at the foreman level. However, the foreman should know what to do in the event of an unsatisfactory adjustment.

In most situations, the employee will express his dissatisfaction to the foreman who then can either restudy the case in an attempt to arrive at a more satisfactory solution or refer the employee to the next higher level of management.

Most companies have policy manuals or union contracts that outline in detail the grievance procedure to be followed by the employee. The foreman is usually (in fact should always be) at the first step. In the event the adjustment is not satisfactory, the employee may take his grievance to the next higher level.

Occasionally, even though the employee does not express it, the alert foreman detects an unsatisfactory adjustment through its effect on other people or on productivity. The foreman should take the initiative in trying another adjustment or suggesting that the employee take his case to the next level of the grievance procedure.

8

METHODS IMPROVEMENT

Production in America has increased tremendously in recent years to a gross national product of $800 to $900 billion of goods and services. Of course, many more people are now working than at any previous point in our history, new and improved equipment has been introduced, and automation is constantly being increased—with even greater advances yet to be made.

But the greatest factor in all this improvement in quantity of output is the increased productivity of each American worker. And this improvement, in turn, is due in large measure to the fundamental belief on the part of production managers and supervisory personnel that "there is always a better way"—a belief that has kept them ever on the alert to find easier and better methods of doing things. This attitude is particularly prevalent among industrial foremen because they are closest to the job being done and the people doing it, and, therefore, are in the position to make the greatest improvement.

There should be no complaint about lack of opportunity today. Fortunes can be made by even small improvements. The fellow who thought of putting an eraser on the end of a pencil probably made more money than Robert Fulton did with his steamboat. However, in order for the foreman to improve methods or systems in his department, he must adopt the basic philosophy that an organized, systematic approach to any job will uncover a better and easier way of doing it than will a haphazard, trial-and-error approach. In other words, a *technique* must be used to make the *philosophy* work.

Scientific management, as it is known today, really started in the 1880's. Frederick W. Taylor is the man who is most often credited with furthering the application of scientific methodology to industry. Together with H. L. Gantt, Harrington Emerson, and others, Taylor developed the questioning, fact-finding techniques which have gradually replaced the old rule-of-thumb procedures. Fifty or sixty years ago, the principles and tools of scientific management, as we know and use them today, were considered revolutionary.

Frank B. Gilbreth and his wife, Lillian M. Gilbreth, were responsible for the development and refinement of the techniques first suggested by Taylor. They were the pioneers in the use of process charts, motion study, and micromotion study. Then, about 1937, Allan H. Mogensen recognized the failure of the "efficiency expert" technique in industrial management and began his search for a nontechnical procedure which could readily be applied by foremen and supervisors on the job by enlisting the wholehearted assistance of the workers. With the help of Erwin H. Schell, David B. Porter, and Lillian M. Gilbreth, Mogensen developed the concept of work simplification, which he defined as "the organized use of common sense to find easier and better ways of doing work."

What Work Simplification Is

Work simplification does not mean, as many have feared, "speedup." Everyone knows that greater production (not productivity) can be gained by simply speeding up the entire operation, but this amounts to speeding up the inefficient and unnecessary elements of the job as well as the necessary. The usual results of such a procedure are worker fatigue and inferior quality. Better methods, through the application of work simplification, result in increased productivity with no extra effort on the part of the worker.

The foreman or the supervisor is the key person in the application of the work simplification technique because he is responsible for the quantity and quality of the work produced. He is responsible for the best use of each employee's present abilities on each job. He is also responsible for the training of new employees and the instruction of old employees on new jobs. No one knows more than the foreman about the "bottlenecks" and "hot spots" in his department which stand in the way of full production. By using the simple analytic tools of work simplification, his knowledge of the job, and the assistance of his employees, he can cut right to the causes of wasted effort and lost motion on the part of his operators.

To be successful in any attempt to improve methods, the foreman must be aware of three characteristics of human nature: (1) Most people resist change or being changed; (2) most people resist the new; and (3) most people resent criticism. Some years ago Charles Kettering said:

> You can send a message around the world in one-seventh of a second, and yet it may take years to force a simple idea through a quarter-inch of human skull; and the slow, creeping, cumulative efforts of years are needed to establish new habits in industry.

The resistance to change is an all-pervasive trait in human nature; it is an emotional reaction, having nothing to do with logic. It increases directly in proportion to the amount of driving used to make the change. In contrast, when a change is made slowly and gradually, and particularly when the workers have contributed something to the change, very few people will resist it or object to it.

Someone once said, "Like a parachute, the mind functions only when it is open." Each foreman should make this test: "When the general foreman or the superintendent introduces a new idea without consulting me, what is my first reaction? Do I immediately start looking for every possible reason or excuse why the new idea won't work, why it cannot be done?" If his first reaction is that it can't be done, that new idea will never work—for him. No matter how clever he is, once he makes up his mind he is through. Someone else, knowing nothing about the problem but believing that it can be solved, will have a greater chance of success. Why? Because he has an open mind.

And, finally, there is the tendency to resent criticism. Suppose a man is criticized for the way he parts his hair, the way he drives his car, or the way he runs his job. His normal reaction is resentment.

There are two kinds of criticism, destructive and constructive. The first is utterly useless and very damaging; the second, if properly used, can be good for anyone. It not only helps a man to do a better job, but it prevents him from making the same mistake a second time.

If constructive criticism is so beneficial, why do most people constantly resent it? Probably because they prefer being told that they are right, which does not happen often enough. When they ask for advice, most people already have an opinion or an idea that they merely want verified. Thus the production foreman must keep in mind that any change in the way an operator is now doing his job can be construed by him as personal criticism. This situation, however, can be avoided or greatly reduced if the operator has played a part in developing the change.

The Five Steps of Work Simplification

1. *Pick the job to improve.* The foreman applying work simplification must first exercise good judgment in the selection of the operations to be studied. Since there are probably many operations in his department requiring study, he should give preference to those where improvement will have the greatest effect and the greatest chance of early success. As Professor Mullee of New York University states:

> Use the steam shovel approach to do the most good and take out the biggest bites—After Work Simplification has been effectively used for some time, get down to the hand shovel, and finally down to the teaspoon.

The following list will help to identify some of the operations the foreman should consider first:

- "Bottlenecks"—operations retarding the flow of work. Work piles up in a particular spot while other people are waiting.
- Waste—operations producing a great deal of scrap or rejects. Skilled people do unskilled work.

- Backtracking—operations where materials or operators do excessive moving back and forth between points, causing people to chase around looking for tools, materials, or other things that ought to be handy.
- Too much handling—operations where excessive transfer of materials is taking place.
- Workload inequities—operations where individual workloads are out of balance.

Every job in the plant (or a do-it-yourself job at home) can be broken down into the following steps:

- *Make ready.* This is the time and effort required to prepare to do the job—in other words, everything leading up to the actual operation. This usually adds only cost, no value, to the product.
- *Do.* This is the actual doing of the operation. This does add value.
- *Put away.* This is the remaining part of the job, such as removal of material from machine, cleaning up, and so on. This again adds no value—only expense.

Although the "do" part is the prime objective of any operation, it often consumes less than 50 percent of the overall time. Somehow, perhaps through habit, greater emphasis is placed on the "do" part of each operation than on the "make ready" and "put away." By concentrating a little more on the other two parts, the foreman not only will be paying attention to a very large portion of the operation, but will be training his sights on those areas where the greatest cost and fatigue are very often found.

2. *Break down the job.* This step gets right down to the bedrock of how to eliminate waste and improve methods.

In order to study a complete job, every detail must be listed exactly as it is now being done. Each move that is made—what is carried, how far it is carried, how long it waits, and when it is inspected—must be identified and set down for further study. This is the phase of the organized plan which could be called making a "still photograph" that can be analyzed in the search for possible improvements.

This step adheres to the basic philosophy of applied common sense in at least two respects: (*a*) It is almost impossible to plot a course to the next point unless and until the present location and conditions are known; and (*b*) attention can be directed to only one thing at a time (most jobs and operations are too complex to be studied as a whole).

The breakdown of the job may be made on a piece of paper from a plain scratch pad as long as each step of the process is written down in its proper order. However, a better job will be done if a flow process chart (see Exhibit 10) is developed and used.

A flow process chart is a step-by-step account of everything that takes place during an operation or procedure. It also includes other desirable information for analysis, such as time required and distance moved. Flow process charts are referred to as either material or operator charts. The *material* type presents the process in terms of what happens to the material. The *operator* type presents the process in terms of the activities of the operator.

There are a few simple rules to be followed when developing a flow process chart on the form supplied for this purpose:

a. Write in the name of the operation or job to be studied.
b. Indicate whether it is to be an *operator* or a *material* chart. (Make sure you keep to the same type all the way through.)
c. Indicate whether the *present* or a *proposed* method is being written up.
d. Write a brief, telegraphic description of each step in the operation.
e. Show other necessary information, such as approximate distance moved and the time involved.
f. Select an appropriate symbol for each step and draw a connecting line from one to the other.

For purposes of clarity, the chart should always have a definite starting point and a definite finishing point; it should bring into the picture only those details which are actually a part of the job in question. For example, if the job is that of a man feeding his dog, it must contain only those of his actions which are directly related to feeding the dog. If, occasionally, he stops to light a cigarette, that is not a part of the job. Similarly, if, after he has fed the dog and put

Exhibit 10

Flow Process Chart

JOB _____

SUBJECT CHARTED _____

CHARTED BY _____

DATE _____

DEPT. _____

SUMMARY

METHOD	PRES.	PROP'D.	SAVG.
NO. OF OPERATIONS			
NO. OF TRANSPORTATIONS			
NO. OF STORAGES			
NO. OF INSPECTIONS			
MAN HOURS OR MINUTES			
DISTANCE TRAVELED			

DETAILS (PRESENT / PROPOSED) METHOD	OPER.	TRANS.	STORAGE	INSPECT.	DIST. IN FEET	TIME IN MINUTES	WHAT?	WHERE?	WHEN?	WHO?	HOW?	NOTES
	○	○	▷	☐					WHY?			
	○	○	▷	☐								

away the things which he used in the process, he decides to take a walk, that is not a proper subject for analysis.

This, then, is the distinction: Anything that belongs to the regular routine of doing a given job, even though it is unrelated to that job, should appear on the chart. Irrelevancies should not be charted. In the example just cited, lighting a cigarette should be included if it is a part of the man's regular routine but should be omitted if it is only an occasional action.

For analytical purposes and as an aid in detecting and eliminating inefficiencies, it is convenient to classify the actions which occur during a given process under four headings—*operation, transportation, inspection,* and *storage.*

Operation. An operation occurs whenever an object is intentionally changed in any of its physical or chemical characteristics, is assembled or disassembled from another object, or is arranged or prepared for another operation or for transportation, inspection, or storage. An operation also occurs whenever information is given or received or whenever planning or calculating takes place. The actions of picking up an object, driving a nail, putting the nut on a bolt, and sorting mail are all operations.

Transportation. A transportation occurs when an object is moved from one place to another, except when such a movement is part of an operation or is caused by the operator of the work station during an operation inspection. Examples of transportations are the following: a letter being carried from one desk to another by messenger, material being moved by truck from one department to another, a product being transported from one building to another by conveyor.

Inspection. An inspection occurs when an object is examined for identification or is verified for quality or quantity in any of its characteristics. Examples of inspections are these: inspecting a product for flaws, verifying quantities of raw materials received, proofreading a letter, checking extensions on invoices.

Storage. A storage occurs when an object is kept and protected against unauthorized removal. The storage symbol also is used to designate delay. A delay occurs when conditions do not permit the performance of the next operation or inspection. This step was known for many years as a "temporary storage."

Frequently, the chart alone does not give a sufficiently detailed picture of the job. In such instances, an illustration such as a floor diagram, a drawing of a tool or setup, or whatever explanation is required should accompany the chart.

When any operation is investigated in sufficient detail to result in a complete flow process chart, suggestions for operation improvement are bound to occur to the person making the chart. The process chart reverses the usual procedure in any job study. Instead of changing a subdivision of a process merely because that particular subdivision is the easiest to change or the one offering the greatest opportunity for improvement, it considers all those acts preceding and following the subdivision. Unless these are all considered, the changes made may secure only a part of the possible benefits and may not be in the best interests of the operation as a whole.

There are several important things for the foreman to remember when making a flow process chart.

- Generally, try to chart a complete cycle. If the chart starts with the worker leaving his bench to perform some task, it should follow him through the complete cycle and end with his return to his bench.
- Do not attempt to cover too much ground.
- Do not draw a flow process chart while sitting at a desk. It can only be done while actually watching the worker perform all the various steps.
- Be sure every operation, transportation, storage, and inspection is shown, no matter how brief these steps may be.
- Keep the subject clearly in mind. If the chart is of a material, for example, it should not include details which affect only the operator.
- Do not worry about the accuracy of distances traveled unless they are important factors in the study of the job.
- Do not assume that a chart needs to be elaborate. Time should not be wasted on appearances. Any diagrams or sketches included should only be sufficiently clear to serve the purpose.
- Define the make ready and put away operations as clearly as possible. They are usually responsible for waste.
- Consider weighing a combination of an operation and a quantity inspection.

- In charting a person, show transportation only if he takes more than one step from the workplace.

3. *Question every detail.* The questioning attitude is the key to all methods improvement and therefore is essential to everyone engaged in that work. Moreover, an open mind must be maintained throughout the questioning of each step of a process or procedure. It should never be assumed that a step is necessary and that the methods used are the best and most economical.

An operation is analyzed by applying a questioning attitude to all the factors affecting it. Many years ago, Rudyard Kipling wrote a poem containing these often-quoted words:

> I keep six honest serving men,
> (They taught me all I knew)
> Their names are Why and What and When
> And How and Where and Who.

These same six "serving men" are used during the analysis phase of studying a process or procedure to direct the thinking and imagination. The first question to ask is, "Why is the job being done at all?" The fact that it is being done does not mean that it is necessary. A lot of time has been spent improving jobs that did not really have to be done in the first place. However, if it is decided that the job is necessary, each detail should be questioned, step by step, as follows.

The foreman should first ask these "why" questions: Why is this step necessary? What would happen if it weren't done? Is there a good reason for doing this?

Here the answer may be, "We have done it that way for years." One of our leading industrial executives, however, takes this view: "A job done the same way for six months would make me question it. When done the same way for a year, I am then sure it's being done the wrong way."

Most managers today feel that the longer a job has been done in a particular way, the more susceptible it is to change.

The foreman then asks the "what" questions: What is the purpose of this step? What is being done? What does this add to the product? (Note that transportation and transferring add nothing.)

Next come the "where" questions: Where is this being done? Where else might this be done? Why should it be done here? And the "when" questions: When is this work done? When is the best time to do it? (Should the sequence be changed or should this step be combined with some other?)

Now the foreman turns to the problem of "who": Who does this item? Who else might do it? Should the person be skilled or unskilled? Is special training required? And, finally, he asks the "how" questions: How is this item done? What other methods might be tried? Is this the simplest way to do it? Should we request a methods study?

There are a number of other questions which, in the past, have led to improvements. A periodic review of these questions by the foreman or supervisor is therefore suggested as an aid to sharpening up this tool. The questions are listed according to operation component.

a. Materials

- Can cheaper material be substituted?
- Is the material uniform and in proper condition when brought to the operator?
- Is the material of proper size, weight, and finish for the most economical use?
- Is the material utilized to the fullest extent?
- Can some use be found for scrap and rejects?
- Can the number of storages of material and of parts in process be reduced?

b. Materials handling

- Can the number of times the material is handled be reduced?
- Can the distance involved be shortened?
- Is the material received, moved, and stored in suitable containers? Are the containers kept clean?
- Can transfer of material from one container to another be reduced?
- Are there delays in the delivery of material to the operator?
- Can the operator be relieved of handling materials by the use of conveyors or other means?
- Can backtracking be reduced or eliminated?

- Will a rearrangement of the layout or a combination of operations make it unnecessary to move the material?

c. *Fixtures and holders*

- Can fixtures or holders be changed so that less skill is required to perform the operation?
- Are both hands occupied by productive work in using fixtures or other equipment?
- Can a simpler device be used?
- Can the variety of bobbins or spools be reduced?
- Could one or two standard sizes be used?
- Can any operation be eliminated through a minor design change in a previous operation?

d. *Machine*

(1) *Setup*
- Should the operator set up his own machine?
- Can the number of setups be reduced by proper lot sizes?
- Are patterns, tools, and gauges obtained without delay?
- Are there production delays during inspection?

(2) *Operation*
- Can the operation be eliminated?
- Can the work be done in multiple?
- Can the machine output be increased?
- Can an automatic device be used?
- Can the operation be divided into two or more short operations?
- Can two or more short operations be combined into one?
- Can the sequence of the operation be changed?
- Can the amount of spoiled work be reduced?
- Can any pre-positioning be done for the next operation?
- Can interruptions be reduced or eliminated?
- Can an inspection be combined with an operation?
- Is the machine in good condition?

e. *Operator*

- Is the operator qualified mentally and physically to perform this operation?

- Can unnecessary fatigue be eliminated by a change in tools, fixtures, layout, or working conditions?
- Can the operator's performance be improved by further instruction?

4. *Develop the improved method.* During the development of an improved method, the foreman must refer to the flow process chart that shows the present method. The six groups of questions previously listed should then be applied to each step of the process or procedure. Reference should also be made at this time to the layout flow diagram, if one has been made, as an aid in determining if there is any unnecessary traveling. When the questions are applied in proper sequence, the analyst will probably make suggestions in the following order:

a. Can the operation be eliminated? What? Why? Sometimes time is spent improving operations which are later found to be unnecessary. The foreman may eventually decide to eliminate the step under analysis in the process.

b. Can it be combined? Where? When? Who? If the step in the operation cannot be eliminated, an attempt should be made to combine it with another. Combined steps utilize men and machines better by performing two or more former steps at the same time.

c. Can the sequence be changed? Where? When? Who? There is a logical pattern to follow in doing any job. When this pattern is not followed, time and money are usually lost. For example, when an inspection is out of sequence, the cost of rejects at that point may be unnecessarily high as a result of additional operations performed on substandard work, which is then rejected after inspection at a later point in the process. Operations out of sequence can also cause unnecessary travel.

d. Can it be simplified? How? The present method used in each step should be questioned. Ask how this work is being done. Can it be simplified, or is the best method now being used? When developing methods improvements, there is occasionally a tendency to ignore any and all costs involved. Remember that proposed methods changes are usually more acceptable to the boss when their costs are moderate.

After completing the analysis of the present method, the foreman should prepare a flow process chart and layout flow diagram of his proposed method, referring to his check marks and notes on the present flow process chart. The new documents, when completed, will enable him to present his proposed methods changes in a form that can be easily understood by anyone in the company.

5. *Apply the new method.* Before the new method can be used, it may have to be "sold" to other people up and down the line. Therefore, its written description should clearly indicate what it will do—cost savings, time, effort, additional safety, and other advantages. Be sure to give credit to any other person contributing to it.

And remember that the new method is not necessarily permanent. The new way of today will become the old method of tomorrow.

The Human Side

William J. Reilly, in his book *The Law of Intelligent Action,* says

> When a person is confronted with a problem, the intelligence of his action is dependent on three primary factors: (1) his *desire* to solve the problem, (2) his *ability* to solve the problem, and (3) his *capacity* for handling the human relations involved.*

In regard to Reilly's first point, one may well ask, "Do most supervisors want to find answers to their problems?" Of course they do, if they intend to be successful. They must encourage their workers to feel, as most people do, that they can gain something by helping their supervisors arrive at solutions to their problems more quickly and accurately.

Do people also have the ability to help solve the supervisor's problems? In many cases, tremendous ability has developed in the proper management *climate.* Men can be placed in departments or divisions and classified according to skill and ability, but brains can't be departmentalized or classified. Brains are where you find them!

As for Reilly's third point, it is human nature to resist change and to resent criticism, and, unfortunately, most work improvement

---

* Harper & Row, Publishers, Inc., New York, 1945.

programs do represent a change for many people and criticism for a few.

The gyroscope is a marvelous example of resistance to sudden change. It will resist a sudden change in position so strongly that it may even be destroyed, but its position can be completely changed if the operation is performed slowly.

As was explained in the previous chapter, most people do not like to be criticized no matter how constructive the criticism is. Even when we ask for criticism, we most often really want praise. If a man says to his wife, "I just waxed the car. Come on out and take a look at it and tell me what you think," and she says, "Good job! Shines like a new dime," everything is fine. On the other hand, if she tells the truth and says that it's streaky, the man will dig up 20 reasons to justify the poor job.

Consultation with the people involved is a real help in job improvement, particularly in the questioning stage. True consultation, however, involves a definite philosophy which attempts the following tasks:

- Seeking sincerely for ideas, reactions, and feelings.
- Recognizing each employee's importance.
- Sharing information, ideas, plans, and problems with the people involved.
- Recognizing that the employee knows more about his job than anyone else does.

Consultation is not:

- Selling ideas under a disguise.
- Going through the motions of letting other people talk without paying attention to their reactions.

The foreman should ask himself, "Who will have to accept any improvement before it can work? My supervisor? My employees? The man who signs the checks?" He must then get these people interested and help them to realize that a problem exists and that their contributions toward its solution will be recognized and appreciated.

No one can resist a new idea when it is partly his or feel criti-

Exhibit 11

Rules for Motion Economy

Motions should be productive.

Motions should bring the end result closer. Hands should not hold anything, but be released for productive work.

Motions should be rhythmic and smooth.

Arrange the work to take advantage of natural, easy rhythm.

Motions should be simple.

The fewest number of body members (and the easiest to use) should be employed. Motions should follow curved rather than straight paths where possible.

Workers should be comfortable.

Chair, table height, lighting, and work layout should be so arranged that the person doing the job can work in comfort, either sitting or standing.

Combine tools whenever possible.

It is usually quicker to turn a small "two-ended" tool end for end than it is to lay one tool down and pick up another (for example, an eraser on the end of a pencil).

Pre-position tools and materials.

A holder should permit the tool to be grasped in the manner in which it will be held while in use (see a fountain pen desk set).

Horizontal

Locate work in normal work areas.

Avoid long reaches and stretches in awkward positions.

Vertical

Use gravity wherever possible.

Gravity-feed bins and containers should be used to deliver material to the point of use or assembly.

cized when asked to adopt a new plan if he has helped to develop it.

We do not have to be geniuses (or even engineers) to be imaginative enough to work out simple job improvements. Some supervisors waste time waiting for the spectacular, earth-shaking improvement that will make thousands of dollars for themselves and their company. In the meantime, many others are out looking for the little improvements—the "five and dime" ideas which will save seconds here or a minute there. Frequently the same man who is looking for the little ideas gets the big ideas too. Even if he doesn't, little ideas for improvement add up to production miracles and result in success for the supervisor.

Motion Economy

Many of these "little ideas" are the fruits of a sound knowledge of motion study techniques. The secret of being economical of motion lies in being "motion-minded"—that is, having the habit of constantly asking: "How can this job be done with less physical or mental effort?" Exhibit 11 presents points to remember that may help.

9

SAFETY AND ACCIDENT PREVENTION

THE SAFETY MOVEMENT in American industry began around the turn of the century. Probably no other topic has been the subject of so many lectures, campaigns, meetings, conferences, and such widespread publicity. Yet accidents occur every day, often with injuries or even loss of life.

Safety is an ever-present problem for the foreman, and his work in this area is never completed. Each day he enters his department, he is responsible for seeing that his people are satisfactorily protected on the job and that they work in a safe manner. There are frequent incidents that the foreman must record as accidents even though no one is hurt.

For example, the shirt sleeve of a lathe operator becomes loose and gets caught in the chuck. In a flash, the sleeve is torn from the shirt and continues to whirl around with the chuck. The operator is not hurt, and there is no damage to the lathe. This is clearly an accident because the operator certainly did not expect it to happen. It should be reported and investigated because serious injury could have occurred.

Since the foreman is responsible for the safety of his employees at all times, he is responsible for all accidents. Accidents not only cause individual workers to lose time but cause the whole workforce to slow down (especially after a serious accident) out of apprehension and excessive caution. The foreman with a good production record usually has a good safety record.

The foreman's general safety responsibilities include training, follow-up, the correction of hazardous conditions, and the setting of an example to the employees of safe work practices.

While the foreman must take the responsibility for accidents in his department, he cannot always be blamed for them. Accidents usually occur because of lack of foresight, and if the foreman exercises due foresight in the effort to anticipate work hazards and an accident still occurs, he is responsible but not necessarily to blame. He should be blamed only when he is found to have been wrong or negligent. For example, if a foreman tells an employee to use a machine from which he knows that a guard has been removed, he is not only responsible but at fault should an accident happen.

Mechanical and Physical Causes

There are several basic causes of accidents to which the foreman should be alert. The following conditions can be grouped as *mechanical causes*: A machine itself can lack guards, be improperly designed, operate at too high speeds, operate under a load that is too heavy for it, or suffer from inadequate maintenance. Tools can be defective in design, worn out or obsolete, makeshift (used for jobs for which they were not designed), or, again, improperly maintained. Lack of proper equipment and hazardous arrangement of equipment also can be added to the list of mechanical causes of accidents.

To correct such mechanical conditions, the foreman must be continually on the watch; he should inspect all tools and equipment periodically. He should see that machines are properly guarded at all times to the point of stopping their operation until they *are* guarded, and he should also insist on the proper maintenance of all tools and equipment. Also, the foreman should be alert to new hazards as conditions change and take the necessary preventive action.

There are, in addition, *physical causes* of accidents involving materials and conditions in the workplace. Materials may fall or roll if they are improperly stacked or stored. Inflammable materials need extra care in their safeguarding. The following physical conditions in the workplace are often causes of accidents: poor housekeeping, congestion, overhead obstructions, accumulation of excessive scrap near workplaces, inadequate light and ventilation, dirty or wet floors, and electrical hazards.

The foreman must understand the hazards associated with materials and working conditions in order to call these hazards to the attention of his employees. Again, he must inspect the storage of materials and combustibles, check the lighting and ventilation, and insist on good housekeeping, clear aisles, and dry floors. In general, he has to spot violations of the rules promptly and either correct them himself or report them to the proper authority.

While management, through the foremen, is reponsible for insuring safe working conditions, guarding machines, providing good equipment and tools, teaching safe work methods, and giving adequate safety supervision, the worker shares in the responsibility of protecting himself and other workers. If he is permanently or partly disabled, he will undoubtedly suffer a reduction in earning power and probably have to reduce his standard of living.

The Element of Human Failure

Despite all of management's efforts, the failure of the human element still causes many accidents. Involved here is the mental, emotional, and physical condition of the employee. How he thinks and feels about his job and his off-the-job environment and whether he is in good health, is sick, or has a physical defect have a direct bearing on his ability or desire to observe safe practices on the job. Physical safeguarding of equipment alone does not solve the problem.

One of the main causes of accidents at work is the employee's disregard of instructions. He may never have received adequate instruction in the first place, he may be overconfident, careless, or uninterested in a monotonous job. Of course, if he has a generally negative attitude, he will tend to find all kinds of fault with his instructions and never become sold on safety. It is poor supervision that allows unsafe work practices to develop into habits.

Another human factor is the mental state of the worker. The greatest single element is worry, whether about home conditions, sickness in the family, finances, or job insecurity. Similarly important is resentment. A man may be brooding over some disciplinary step which was particularly tactless, and, when an employee's mind is preoccupied with such matters, he cannot give full attention to his work.

Physical defects—usually in sight or hearing—can also cause accidents. A worker may suffer from other deformities as well, either known or unknown to him. The sick employee is always accident-prone. Then, too, some workers are improperly placed; they may be too tall or too short for the job; they may not be strong enough; or they may lack endurance. Moreover, as the pace of industrial production increases and automation grows, the employee's reaction time becomes increasingly important in many jobs.

The foreman has to be very discerning to offset the human causes of accidents. He must carefully analyze any disregard of instructions and any instance of carelessness. The employee may have a real or imaginary grievance which needs attention. Even the off-the-job problems for the worker become on-the-job problems for the foreman—problems that may require counseling and increased supervision for a while. When the foreman encounters physical defects in one of his subordinates, he may have to transfer him to another job where the defect will not affect his work or endanger his safety and that of others. In general, the foreman should be thoroughly informed on all human causes of accidents so that he can anticipate the conditions which will make a worker accident-prone and correct them before an accident happens.

Accident Investigation

The foreman must investigate all accidents, whether or not they result in an injury, to determine the cause or causes and take immediate corrective action. Certain specific procedures for investigating accidents should be established either by and for the company as a whole or by the foreman for himself. A suggested procedure follows:

1. Interview worker or workers directly involved.
2. Interview witnesses.
3. Carefully check the place of the accident.
4. Carefully inspect tools, machine, equipment, and any other items involved in the accident.
5. Determine the primary cause—mechanical, physical, or human.
6. Take immediate corrective action.
7. Inform all employees of the details of the accident and the corrective action taken.

Exhibit 12 is a suggested chart on which the foreman can fill in the results of his investigation.

Good management of the safety function by the foreman requires that all accidents be reported as well as investigated. Most insurance companies provide forms for reporting accidents, or the company or the foreman can make up one in terms of the data that the insurance company wants. In any case, a report should be made of the accident and kept in the employee's file. The report form should be completed *regardless* of whether anyone was injured. Minor injuries, when not properly treated, may develop into more serious cases. Accidents which do not cause personal injury may, if they are not investigated and reported and the hazard is not corrected, occur again with more serious consequences. Exhibit 13 is a suggested accident report form for the foreman's convenience.

Despite all the policing—the demands of the company and the foreman that every accident be reported—some employees will always be reluctant to do so when an incident results in only minor injury or no injury or property damage. The reasons sometimes given for this reluctance are:

1. Fear of having one's personal accident record show a higher rate and act as a demerit.
2. Fear of loss of income while disabled.

(*text continues on page 128*)

Exhibit 12

Accident Investigation Procedure

Accident:

---

1. Statement by injured worker:

2. Statements by witnesses:

3. Results of check of place of accident:

4. Results of check of tools, machines, equipment, and other items involved:

5. Was primary cause mechanical, physical, or human?

6. Corrective action taken:

7. Steps taken to inform all workers of accident and corrective action:

Exhibit 13

Suggested Accident Report Form

_____ _____ _____A.M./P.M
     (Department)   (Date)   (Time)

Date of accident _____ 19__   Hour of day _____

Worker's name _____   Identification No. _____

Address _____   Age ____ Occupation _____

Nature of work at time of accident _____

Nature of injury _____

_____

Cause of accident _____

_____

How could this accident have been prevented? _____

_____

Was worker given first aid? ____   Was worker sent to doctor? ____

Name of first-aid man _____   Address _____

Type of first aid given _____

   Witnesses to accident:

Name _____   Address _____

Name _____   Address _____

Was injured worker able to return to regular work on his next regular shift? _____

The foregoing statements are true as here reported.

_____ _____
    (Injured Employee)   (Foreman)

3. Inconvenience of getting medical treatment.
4. Lack of confidence in the company doctor or nurse.

In such cases, the foreman may take the following actions:

1. Impress upon the worker that minor injuries, if not reported and treated immediately, may develop complications and result in a permanent disability.
2. Point out that failure to report accidents which do not result in injury or property damage will only mean that the hazard will continue to exist, and may cause injury to other workers or serious damage to equipment.
3. Give increased supervision to the employee suspected of not reporting accidents.
4. When these methods fail, administer discipline in the degree required.

To further overcome reluctance of workers to report all accidents, the foreman should—

1. Strive for a good accident record in fact and not on paper only. The latter will only encourage workers to conceal accidents.
2. Put the accident-report problem squarely up to the workers and enlist their cooperation. In the long run, this should get results.
3. If the company does not pay workers on accident disability an amount large enough to supplement compensation payments, point out to management the desirability of such a policy.

An On-Going Program

Safety work should be a constant, vital activity. But, like many functions, it is sometimes allowed to degenerate into an intermittent program which only comes to light immediately after a serious accident.

Actually, in order to promote a good safety program and keep it alive, a safety committee should be organized. A safety committee will provide safety education for its members and perform certain executive duties such as determining standards for guarding machines and equipment, developing safety rules, investigating all accidents and deciding what must be done to prevent their recurrence, and reviewing all safety suggestions and recommendations and deciding upon their practicability. A safety committee encourages an active safety-consciousness in all employees and helps to eliminate hazards and maintain good plant housekeeping.

The size of the company and the nature of its business will decide the size and composition of the committee. A typical group might include the plant manager, the superintendent, the personnel director, one or more foremen, and one or more employees. In the case of foremen and employees, different people can serve through a quarterly or semi-annual rotation system, while the others named can serve as permanent members. In no case should the committee consist of fewer than three members.

In some organizations where regular meetings of foremen are held, the chairman of the safety committee or the plant safety director participates. The work of the safety committee may be part of the work of the foreman group as a whole. This allows all foremen to attend these meetings and share in the discussions; safety thus becomes integrated into their regular activities. The larger insurance carriers have a staff of people ready to assist a company in setting up such meeting discussions, and they have an abundance of material in the way of movies, slides, posters, and so on to be used for educational purposes. The National Safety Council will provide similar aids.

Since all states have a workmen's compensation system where costs are charged to the employer as a part of the cost of doing business, the foreman should have a working knowledge of the particular act that affects him. The workmen's compensation laws undergo constant study and revision, and not all have the same provisions. In one state, failure of an employer to comply with statutes regarding safety devices may increase compensation by 15 percent, while willful failure of an employee to use such devices may reduce compensation by 15 percent.

In conclusion, the following points should be remembered:

1. Accidents can be prevented by the intelligent use of modern accident prevention practices.
2. The foreman is responsible for accidents in his department and should continually be on the alert to detect and correct hazards.
3. The foreman should train his force in safe working practices and continually urge them by every available management device to become and remain safety-minded.
4. The foreman should set a good example in safe work habits.
5. The foreman should become an active member of the plant safety committee where one exists or do his best to convince management to institute such a committee.
6. The foreman should take advantage of any and all educational courses or lectures in safety that are available.
7. The foreman should become acquainted with the requirement of his state's Workmen's Compensation Act.

10

A CONSTRUCTIVE
CORRECTION PROCEDURE

An old, easy, and false statement holds that it is easy to criticize. But it is not easy to criticize in a constructive manner. If it were, more people would do it. The truth is that many foremen, like anyone else, are reluctant to speak up; they hesitate to criticize substandard work, attitudes, or habits. This is not only because the subordinates' feelings may be hurt but also because the supervisor naturally recoils from an unpleasant task.

And yet this task must be done. It is understood in the employer–employee relationship at the point of hire that the employer's representative (supervisor, department manager, or foreman) will bring to the employee's attention any defection from standard. Furthermore, the supervisor should do it as soon and as cordially, helpfully, and constructively as possible. Unless he makes this effort, he is not really a manager.

The Implicit Employer–Employee Agreement

Many procedures for the selection and hiring of people are lengthy, comprehensive, and generally excellent. Such a procedure may be applied to a small or a large number of men, depending upon the job which is to be filled and the number of people applying for it. At the same time, a man out of a job or currently employed but looking for another employer may find himself actually in the position of having to choose from a number of companies before he finds the one which suits him best. This is especially true in a tight labor market in which jobs are plentiful and talent is relatively scarce. Regardless of the number of applicants the company screens, however, and the number of opportunities the man looks into, at some point man and company must come together—he as the employee and the company as the employer. At that moment, the two parties enter into an agreement without either party's uttering a word. They have an implicit understanding which lasts as long as the employee and the employer stay together.

This agreement is never put in writing and signed by both parties, and it is not a legally enforceable instrument. Nonetheless, it exists as part of the moral code of both employee and employer, and, unfortunately, it is violated at times—more often by the employer than by the employee. It is therefore important that each foreman understand this agreement because he is the person who represents the company to the employee and so must live in accordance with the agreement.

This is what each party agrees to before any work actually gets under way:

The employee says:
1. I like this company and the people I have met here. I would like to work for them in the job which is open.
2. I will work diligently and give a good day's work for a good day's pay.
3. Although I may have held similar jobs before, I have never worked at this job for this company.
4. This company, as does every company, has its own rules, policies, codes of behavior, and standards of performance, and I expect that, in my induction and early training, it will acquaint me with them.
5. In doing my work, I shall try to conform to the company's rules, policies, and codes of behavior and to meet its standards of performance.

6. In the event that I fail to comply with all these rules, policies, and codes of behavior or fall short of the company's standards of performance, I expect that my foreman will immediately bring it to my attention in a constructive manner so as to help me behave or perform as expected.
7. However, if at any time I decide that I do not *want* to conform to or meet the company's standards, or if I become convinced that I *cannot* conform to or meet these standards, I shall feel free to exercise my American worker's right to quit.

The company, through its representative, says:

1. We like what we see in you and believe that we would like to employ you for the job we have open.
2. We expect that you will work diligently and that you will give a good day's work for a good day's pay.
3. We realize that you are a man who is qualified for the job, but we also realize that you have never worked at this job for this company.
4. We have our own rules, policies, codes of behavior, and standards of performance, and we realize that we are obliged to acquaint you fully with all of them.
5. We expect that you will make every effort to conform to the company's rules, policies, and codes of behavior and meet its standards of performance.
6. In the event that you fail to comply with all these rules, policies, and codes of behavior or fall short of the company's standards of performance, your immediate superior will, as soon as the situation is discernible to him, bring it to your attention in a constructive manner so as to help you rectify it.
7. Your supervisor may repeat this sort of constructive correction one or more times, depending upon your effort to conform and upon the gravity of the matter.
8. If, however, after one or more attempts you are still not conforming to or meeting the company standards and your superior is satisfied that he has fulfilled the company's obligation in that regard, he will ask you to leave the company as a discharged employee.

The Foreman's Objectives

A sound philosophy of constructive correction can only exist where management is concerned with consequences. All management personnel, from the chief executive to the line foreman, must be willing to look at results while remaining alert to new methods which might produce even better results.

The first objective of constructive correction, therefore, should always be the *development of the employee*. Greater self-development can be expected when the employee understands what is expected of him, fully recognizes his own need for development, and has participated in developing a plan or at least accepted one which he can follow successfully. Thus the primary job of the supervisor is to help the employee recognize his need for correction or improvement and to make plans for his improvement. It is important to remember that the supervisor can only provide the opportunities for improvement; the employee must make the improvements himself.

The second objective of constructive correction is to maintain or build good employee relations. The results will depend heavily upon the conduct of the discussion.

What Not to Do

To gain only one of the two objectives without the other is not enough. The foreman can resort to the old, ineffective technique of bawling a man out (preferably in front of others so as to make an example of him). This technique may well get improved performance for a while, but only at the tremendous price of damaged employee relations.

On the other hand, the foreman can "look the other way" and do nothing. However, he will get no improvement from that particular employee, while others will feel free to perform in the same substandard manner. The passage of time will make it increasingly difficult to ever do anything about it, and ultimately even the good employees' behavior will degenerate. Most people know a weak foreman when they see one and, for the long pull, they would prefer not to work for one.

Preliminary Considerations

To gain both objectives poses a problem and requires intelligence, planning, and a general procedure to follow. Looking at the pattern horizontally, we can discern four separate steps:

1. The foreman states the problem.
2. He gets the employee's reaction.
3. The two parties consider appropriate action.
4. They evolve and agree to a plan.

Each of the above four stages will be amplified later in this chapter. Before the first stage takes place, however, there are a number of elements which the foreman must seriously consider. This preparation frequently consumes large amounts of time and energy; but, carefully done, it usually returns great dividends.

These are the preliminary considerations:

Facts. Is there an actual problem with this employee or a weakness to be strengthened? Do the records and data available support it? If the problem is absenteeism, specifically when was the employee absent, how many times, and what percentage of the time over a given work period?

The foreman may find that if he has all the facts, the correct answer and action may be obvious. Certainly, without the facts, he cannot intelligently guide the employee. The facts may even show that the employee is not really in need of correction.

Possible causes. What job-connected or outside influences may be causing or contributing to the problem? Is the employee's wife seriously ill? Does he dislike some aspect of his job? In court cases, circumstantial evidence is sometimes more important than eyewitness accounts. However, it takes keen observation to determine whether circumstantial evidence is really factual. In preparation for the discussion, the foreman should go beyond the facts at hand to find out what may be contributing to the situation.

Possible action. At the appropriate time, what suggestion or suggestions can the foreman make to help the employee correct the situation? There is little sense in talking to an employee about a problem if the foreman has no idea of what he or the employee can do about it.

Approach. What kind of person is this employee? Will the fore-man's approach be kid-gloved or rough? Are the time and place right?

Self. Did the foreman himself get out on the right side of bed this morning? If he is upset about this employee or about some other incident of recent occurrence, he should not conduct this dis-cussion, in which anger or irritation can do great harm. Nor should he enter into this kind of interview with a closed mind. He cannot expect to be prosecutor, judge, and jury at the same time.

In addition to these five major areas, of course, there are also many little things to consider before the corrective session. For in-stance, the tone of the foreman's voice, his facial expression, or his mannerisms can make the employee uncomfortable. The foreman should not talk down to the employee, and he should avoid the "let me show you" attitude. Nothing annoys a person more than the sug-gestion that he isn't intelligent enough to grasp the full significance of a situation.

Discussion of the Problem

When all the preliminary steps have been carefully considered and notes made, the foreman is ready to confront the employee with the first phase of the discussion in which he must—

State the problem. The foreman should try to present the prob-lem to the employee so as to get a constructive reaction.

Recognizing the employee's fear of possible bad news, he should quickly come to the point and tell the employe why he has been called in and what the purpose of the interview is. The foreman may use a phrase such as, "I have called you in to talk to you about your job to see if we can improve. . . ." If it is necessary to inform the employee in advance about the discussion, the foreman should also tell him its purpose in advance in order to avoid a growing fear on the part of the employee.

After explaining the purpose of the talk, the foreman should indicate that he recognizes and appreciates the employee's value to the organization. He does this by specifically mentioning some of the employee's good points. If the foreman's statements are based on facts and are not exaggerated, they may help the employee to relax somewhat.

The foreman is now ready to present the problem itself—the employee's weak point or points. The foreman does this in terms of what the employee has done or has failed to do, without indicating what action should be taken about it. The employee's weak points should be stated as *facts,* not as faults.

In this entire first phase, the foreman does all the talking in order to get the whole problem on the table before any discussion of it begins. The foreman presents the problem in an objective fashion, indicating what the record and his own observations have shown. He does not state what he *believes* to be the case, what he *believes* to be the underlying reason, or what he *believes* should be done about it. The foreman is then ready for the second phase, in which he must—

Get the employee's reaction. After having done a good job in the first phase, the foreman will probably get the employee's reaction quite readily. If not, he should encourage the employee to give his side of the story by asking appropriate questions: "Are these facts correct? Have I stated them fairly?"

If the employee agrees with the foreman's statement of the problem, the foreman is ready to move on to the next step. On the other hand, if the employee disagrees, then the foreman will have to consider the nature of the disagreement.

In disagreeing, the employee may indicate that the foreman was incorrect in his statement of the basic facts or that something has been overlooked. If the information presented by the employee is important enough to indicate a possible change in the foreman's thinking, he may need more time for further investigation and study of the problem. Since the employee has introduced new evidence or made a new point, the foreman should give him a "rain check" and postpone the interview until a later date.

However, the foreman may find that in disagreeing the employee does quite a bit of talking but fails to come up with information that seriously alters the case. In such a situation, the foreman may indicate that, while he recognizes the value of the employee's remarks, there are still certain facts which need attention. He may wish to reiterate the weaknesses he has cited and then proceed with the rest of the interview.

When the employee agrees with the basic facts or is unable to offer any material change in the basic facts, the foreman and the employee are ready for the third phase, in which they—

Consider appropriate action. At this point the foreman must humble himself and ask the employee to suggest remedial action. The foreman must honestly want a proposal from the employee. Psychologically, this is a sound procedure, since, if the employee's suggestion can be accepted, the employee will be more willing to follow it. In fact, if the employee's suggestion is satisfactory to the foreman, he can close the interview then and there by agreeing with the employee, stating the plan of action as a reassertion of the employee's suggestion, and assuring the employee that he "will work it out."

The employee may, however, come up with a suggestion that sounds good but has an element in it to which the foreman cannot commit himself immediately. He may have to do some further checking on it—perhaps with his superior or some other supervisor. However, if the foreman recognizes the value of gaining the employee's cooperation, he will take the time necessary to check on the feasibility of the employee's suggestion. In such a case, the foreman postpones the balance of the interview until he can give the employee the results of his investigation.

However, the employee may have no suggestion to offer or he may make impractical suggestions. In either of these situations, the foreman should present his own plan of action. This is the point at which the foreman must draw upon the "possible actions" developed in his preliminary consideration. Here he should indicate what assistance he will give the employee and what assistance will be available from other sources. The employee may readily agree with the foreman's suggestions, or there may be some discussion before full agreement and acceptance are reached.

Before the interview is brought to a close, both the foreman and the employee should clearly understand the plan of action. To this end the foreman should—

State the plan of action. There is a vast difference between a suggestion and a plan. A plan brings the suggestion to life—it has a starting point, checkpoints, a rate of progress, a terminal point, and other features to give it substance. No structure was ever built on just the good idea of the engineer or architect. Plans must be developed on the drawing board.

After the plan of action has been clearly stated and all of its elements are clearly understood, the foreman should terminate the discussion on a note of confidence in the employee by saying, "I'm sure you'll work this out," or, "I know you will try to work this out."

Postinterview Action

So far, the foreman and the employee have just talked. Together they have determined what to do. It is now the job of the foreman to see that the agreed-to plan is put into action and that it accomplishes the desired results. Just as there were things to consider before the interview, there are now steps to be taken.

The foreman may have to initiate the action. Is there any beginning step he has committed himself to? If so, he should take it. Perhaps the employee may need a reminder of when to start. Is the employee off on the right foot? He may need help.

Results are now important. The foreman must observe carefully in order to determine whether the plan of action is the right one in terms of the original objectives of getting corrective action and building or maintaining good employee relations. During the entire follow-up period, the foreman should check the employee's progress once he has had an opportunity to apply the corrective action. The foreman should talk with him again and, if he is doing well, tell him so. If he is failing to carry out his part of the plan, the foreman may have to go through the discussion procedure again.

In this suggested pattern for constructive correction, there are many points at which the foreman has to choose his words carefully. Here are some experience-tested phrases to use with the employee.

When stating the purpose of the discussion, the foreman says, as stated earlier, "I'd like to talk to you about your job to see if we can improve. . . ." He does not conceal what he wants to talk about or go into an involved explanation before the time is right. The suggested phrase also includes the important word "we." The "we" approach should always be used to acknowledge the fact that any problem is a mutual one.

When praising the employee, the foreman can use this phrase: "There are some things you're doing (very) well. . . ." This is part of the foreman's report to the employee on how he is doing. It is stated factually; the foreman does not give praise when praise is not due.

After praise has been given, the foreman can lead up to a discussion of the employee's weak points with the words, "But I'm concerned about these facts. . . ." This is an easy phrase for the foreman to use in order to insure himself that he is sticking to the facts. The question is not one of motive. As far as the foreman is concerned, the employee's motives are good, and the employee will do the right thing if he knows what it is. Thus the foreman compares things which the employee does well with things in which he needs to improve. The foreman should never allow himself or the employee to make comparisons with other employees.

When he wants to get the employee's reaction, the foreman may ask, "Do you agree with these facts?" or, "What's your story?" He is essentially asking if he (the foreman) has interpreted the situation properly. More than a yes or no answer is necessary for a clear understanding of the facts.

If the employee disagrees and makes a point, the foreman can reply, "I'm glad you told me these things; they may change the picture somewhat." The foreman thus recognizes that the employee has given him new facts or a new interpretation of the facts. (This may mean that the foreman had prepared insufficiently for the interview.)

If the employee disagrees but makes no real point, just blows off steam or wanders off on an irrelevant tangent, the foreman can bring the discussion back to earth by stating, "Yes, but there are still certain facts that need attention."

"Do you have any suggestion as to what we can do?" is a good way to elicit a suggestion about the desired course of action from the employee. The foreman realizes that the employee will cooperate fully in carrying out his own suggestions.

"I'm sorry but because of . . . I don't think that would work," is a good way of refusing an impractical suggestion. By saying "Suppose we try . . .?" the foreman tactfully brings out his own suggested course of action. When necessary, he may have to assert his authority to see that the right action is decided upon. The phrase, "I'm sure you'll work this out," closes the interview on a friendly, helpful note.

In cases where the employee introduces new facts or advances a suggested course of action which requires study before proceeding further, a statement such as, "I'll check on this and discuss it with you later," is in order. A definite time for the next discussion should be set. In any event, the foreman should assure the employee that they will definitely get together at a later time.

❋   ❋   ❋

The constructive correction procedure is divided and subdivided as in Exhibit 14:

Exhibit 14

Constructive Correction Procedure

1. Before the discussion. Preliminary considerations include—
   a. Facts.
   b. Probable causes.
   c. Possible actions.
   d. Approach.
   e. Self.

2. During the discussion. The foreman should—
   a. State the problem in a way that will elicit constructive effort toward correction.
   b. Encourage the employee to express his reactions, to talk and perhaps clarify the problem for himself.
   c. Discuss appropriate action with the employee.
   d. State the agreed-upon course of action so that it will be clearly understood.

3. After the discussion. The foreman should—
   a. Initiate action.
   b. Observe results in terms of objectives.
   c. Follow up.

As an afterthought, but as part of the follow-up, a report of each constructive-correction session should be made and placed in the employee's file. Since memories are faulty and one man's word is as good as the next man's, it is best to have a written record of what transpired for future reference. In fact, the written record is the best supporting evidence if a case culminates in discharge after several attempts at correction. When a union attempts to contest a discharge, the written record should answer its questions: "What was the cause?" "When was it first noticed?" and, "What was done about it?"

Certainly, if the employee's out-of-line performance is sufficient to call for a constructive-correction discussion, it is sufficient to warrant documentation.

11

GIVING ORDERS

Management, in which the foreman takes an integral part, has been defined as the activity of getting things done through other people. Regardless of his title (president, vice president, sales manager, superintendent, or foreman), the person in any managerial position is responsible for producing a certain quantity and quality of product or service within a given time and at a certain cost. No one in management can do this alone; he or she must depend upon others; thus he or she must issue instructions or *give orders*.

At the same time, the world in general and the business world in particular have changed considerably in the past several decades and are continuing to change. Industrial changes have been coming at an accelerated rate, and no one knows what the rate of change will be in future years except that it will probably be faster.

Since the end of World War II, growth of organized labor and its emergence as a political force, the national emphasis on freedom, the wider distribution of information through greatly improved electronic communications, and new laws on the statute books of the states and the nation have altered employee attitudes. Regardless of how the foreman may feel personally about recent political and economic changes, he must recognize the degree to which they have influenced his employees. He should understand in particular the fact that workers today are more resentful of the exercise of personal authority over them by anyone who, simply by reason of his superior position, can affect their present or future security.

And yet the foreman must get things done. His own present and future depend upon it. He must carefully reconcile the changing attitudes of his people with his task of getting work done through these same people. He cannot assume that the persons to whom he issues instructions will understand him, and he certainly cannot take for granted that they will follow instructions just because he has issued them.

Range of Possibilities

There is a wide range of possible ways to give instruction, with the greatest variable being the worker who receives them. Some people merely need a brief comment or a suggestion as to what is required, while others require a lengthy and detailed explanation of what is wanted and how to proceed. In short, there is much more to giving instructions than appears at first glance.

In the first place, an order is simply a means to an end. This does not mean that the manner in which the instructions are given is unimportant, but unless the required results are obtained, the order itself has been for naught.

Second, the best results will be obtained when the worker carries the order out willingly. Simply ordering him to do something will usually mean that the job will be done by a sullen, unwilling man who has none of the enthusiasm needed to do the job. The way in which the order is given will directly affect the way in which it is carried out.

Third, the order must be made important to the receiver. Again, the manner in which the order is given is the key factor. An order can never be more important to the worker than it seems to be regarded by the foreman who gives it.

The Order-Giving Process

1. The foreman must first determine that an order is necessary. He must fully grasp the entire situation, what the need is, how great it is, and what must be done.

As part of this first step, the foreman should select the employee who will do the job or, at least, will receive the instruction. The foreman must be certain that this employee has the necessary training, skill, and physical ability to carry out the order in the expected manner. No person can be held responsible for an error if he is not qualified to do the job. A good foreman knows that he may obtain poorer results than the employee's qualifications may warrant, but he can never attain better ones.

Three factors are required for effective order giving, particularly for routine orders. The order must be (1) positive, (2) clear, and (3) courteous.

A good order should not read, for example, "This machine will not be moved to Building No. 22." It is better to make the positive statement, "This machine will remain here." Again, one sentence is usually better than two. To say to a secretary, "I think an original and six copies will be enough. We may not use more than four, but it is easier to make more now than later," is not quite clear. It is better to say, "Miss Jones, will you make an original and six copies, please?" And, since an attempt to be positive and clear may give an impression of brusqueness, courtesy is important.

Other preliminary considerations are whether the order should be given in writing or orally and how detailed it should be. There are certain situations in which the written order is more effective. They occur:

- When orders are transmitted to another location.
- When the worker is slow in understanding or forgetful of details.
- When precise figures or complex details are involved.
- When the worker must be held strictly accountable.
- When the order of operation is important and needs to be followed exactly.
- When a bulletin board can be used for general orders or work assignments.
- When "general orders" or higher authorities are being quoted.
- When company policies or interpretations are being developed.

The detail of the order, either written or oral, is governed by—

- The hazards which may exist.
- The specialization of the job.

- The limits of the worker's experience.
- The need for standard procedures.
- A change in process or equipment.
- A lack of willingness on the part of the employee.
- The order's role in job instruction.

2. The second step in the order-giving process is to decide what kind of order to give. Regardless of whether it is written or oral, it will be one of three types.

The direct order. This is a definite assignment to "do this" or "do that" which must be carried out as expressed. It requires immediate and unquestioning obedience, and because it may be abrupt or harsh, it may provoke resentment. The foreman is totally responsible if the result is less than desired. However, the direct order does have its place:

- When an emergency arises.
- When the worker is indifferent.
- When the worker is careless.
- When the employee refuses to follow safety rules.
- When a man refuses to do as he is told.
- When the worker is a chronic objector or "talker."
- When it is necessary to stop waste.
- When haste is important and the task is simple.

The request. A milder, more tactful order is the request. This is a more democratic way of getting things done. It does not necessarily need to be stated in the form of a question and does not require the use of the word "please." What is, in effect, a request is conveyed by saying, "Let's do this or that," or, "I wish you would see what you can do with this."

Use the request effectively in the following situations:

- When dealing with a touchy, nervous, or sensitive person.
- When trying out a newly assigned man.
- When more cooperation is needed.
- When a little more work is needed.
- When the employee must be interested in his work.
- When speaking to an older or highly experienced man.
- When speaking to the "hard-boiled" man.
- When the employee must do a difficult job in a particular way.

In general, the request has the same effect as the direct order, but it is not so likely to arouse resentment and therefore is usually more acceptable.

The implied or suggested order. This order involves virtually no directions. The foreman discusses the task to be done with the employee without giving him specific instructions. The employee then goes ahead under his own power and does what is needed. For example, the foreman tells his stockroom clerk, "I have ordered 25 new A-136 parts." If, when the parts arrive, the clerk enters them in his records, marks each one, and puts them in their proper place, he has carried out an order without actually having been told to do so. The term "implied" or "suggested," as used here, does not mean that the foreman suggests how the job should be done; he merely suggests that it *should be* done. Such an arrangement approaches that of a partnership.

Of all the types of orders, the implied or suggested form is most dependent on the type of employee. It can most safely be used with fully experienced workers or occasionally—

- When improved methods are sought.
- When workers have a sense of responsibility which can be relied upon.
- When workers are trying to get ahead.
- When a new group of experienced employees is being tried out.
- When a foreman is trying to develop initiative.

The implied or suggested order brings out the principle that the other person should share the thinking. The highest form of foremanship lies in making others lead. However, it is not unusual to find a man who dislikes thinking or doing on his own; even when problems are his responsibility, he waits for the foreman to tackle the hard part of the job. With a man like that, a good phrase to use is, "What you might do, Jack, is . . . ."

There is another type of order that is rarely used but is sometimes necessary. This is the *call for volunteers*, which is usually limited to disagreeable or dangerous work. To get the best results from this "order," the foreman should be ready and willing to help with the task for which the volunteers are requested. This order is usually limited to cases—

- Where the job is dangerous.
- Where the job is disagreeable.
- Where the workload is unusually heavy.
- Where overtime is involved.
- Where a skilled worker is needed for a special job.

It might be argued that the call for volunteers and the implied or suggested order are not really orders as such. This is a matter of semantics; the fact is that both are used to get work done.

The foreman must be alert to the fact that the relationship between him and the receiver of the order is strongly affected, either adversely or favorably, by his words, tone of voice, and actions. An attitude cycle is always set in motion; if this is started on a sour note, unsatisfactory results will follow.

In addition, the facts requiring the issuance of the order should be clearly pointed out. These facts help the employee see where his particular work fits into the overall plan and enable him to carry out his work with a greater feeling of importance and responsibility. Furthermore, explaining the reason for the order removes it from the realm of personal command.

3. The foreman should now be ready to give the order, the third step in the process. In this step, it is important that the employee be clear on (1) what he is to do, and (2) when he is to do it. This means that both parties must speak and understand the same language. It also means that the steps to be followed should be presented in logical order.

The timing of the presentation is essential. An order given by a foreman when he has one arm in the sleeve of his overcoat as he hurries out the door will never seem important to the employee receiving the order. The same would be true if it were the employee who was on his way out. In fact, any order given when either party is "on the fly" will appear less important than it should.

To verify whether the employee receiving the order actually understands the assignment, feedback is necessary. The only valid feedback is that which the foreman obtains by asking questions—who? what? when? where? and sometimes how? and why? Any questions which can be answered by yes or no will usually not provide reliable verification.

4. Since an order is given to get certain results, it should include a statement of the results expected, the fourth step in the

process. If the order is "Reduce the amount of scrap," the foreman will have to accept any reduction, even the slightest, as satisfactory since he has not set any real standard. If, on the other hand, the order is "Reduce the amount of scrap by 5 percent by a specific date," a standard has been established. Every man is entitled to know by what yardstick his performance will be measured. When the foreman informs him of the results expected, he is giving him that.

5. If an order is only a means to an end, then the order-giving process is only half the story at best. The other half, or the fifth step, is the follow-up. This is true in nearly every area of good foremanship. The foreman who assumes that the work will be done with satisfactory results will often get less than satisfactory results or no results at all when it is almost too late to do anything about it. On the other hand, good follow-up makes it possible to detect any departure from the terms of the order soon enough to put the worker back on the beam.

The key to effective follow-up is the right kind and the right amount of it. The foreman who hangs on to an assignment rather than letting the employee to whom he gave it do the job is not following up, he is doing the job. Nor is the foreman following up when he constantly looks over the shoulders of his people. The lack of effective follow-up is the single most glaring weakness in management today.

To correct this weakness, the following suggestions are made:

1. On the basis of expected results, decide how the order is to be followed up. Should records, statistics, observations, inspections or all of these methods be used?
2. Be certain that the facilities required for follow-up are available.
3. Decide how soon and how frequently to follow up. This decision requires a knowledge of employee capabilities.
4. Check progress, not people.
5. Don't skip some assignments and follow up on others. This makes it a guessing game to tell which assignments the foreman is actually interested in.

The order-giving process consists of five major steps listed in Exhibit 15.

Exhibit 15

The Order-Giving Process

Step 1. Check the situation.
  Why is the order needed?
  What qualifications are needed?
  Select the worker who will perform the order.
  Determine the kind of order to be given.

Step 2. Evaluate worker.
  Does he require a direct order, a request, or a suggestion?
  Shall a call for volunteers be used?
  Consider words, tones, and actions.
  Get the facts behind the order.

Step 3. Present the order.
  State what the worker is to do.
  State when it is to be done.
  Put first things first.
  Use words the worker understands.
  Watch the timing.
  Make the order seem important to the worker.
  Verify the reception.

Step 4. State results expected.
  Determine the appropriate yardstick to use.
  Inform the worker of the yardstick.

Step 5. Follow-up.
  Determine the amount and kind.
  Don't assume that the work will be done or done right.
  What is to be used as follow-up?
  Check progress, not people.

Remember that giving orders is only the beginning of a continuing process which does not end until the work covered by the order is completed. Hence, these axioms: An order is only a means to an end; it is the results that are important, and the most successful order produces the best results.

12

MORE EFFECTIVE
COMMUNICATION

IN RECENT YEARS, students of management and practicing managers have been treating industrial communication as though it were something new and apart from the normal management way of life. Almost every management publication has at least one article on the subject.

Why the emphasis on improved communication? Although it is not the answer to *all* personnel and production problems, there is no denying the benefits to be derived from better communication. To say nothing of the time saved, improved communication is certainly basic to creating the proper climate for efficient administration. It is also essential to a good program of preventive maintenance in labor relations. Research studies have shown that there is a direct correlation between employee morale and the degree to which foremen keep their employees informed. These studies also indicate that high production is usually found in a group enjoying good communication—up, down, and laterally. Employees in high-production groups say that their foremen are easy to talk to; these foremen tell them where the worker stands and freely explain the reasons behind possible changes in personnel or schedules.

There is always communication in one form or another. There is always a grapevine ready to carry a version of an important happening; the "locker-room lawyer" has all the answers at his fingertips; and the union, when there is one, will offer its interpretation of any controversial issue. The question, then, is not, "Is there any communication?" but, "How can communication be improved?"

Communication as Understanding

Communication has been defined as "the passing of information and understanding from one person to another." This definition points up important elements of communication. First, more than one person is involved; there is always the transmitting party, or the sender, and there must be one or more receivers. Communication involves the transmission of information; however, if the information received is not understood, the communication has not been effective. A man alone on a desert island, calling for help as loudly as he can, is not communicating because there is no receiver. Even if his calls were to bring people to him, there would still be no communication if they did not know his language.

It is relatively simple to make people hear, but it is quite another matter to make them understand. In fact, no one can be *made* to understand. Understanding is personal and subjective. Understanding can occur only in the receiver's mind.

A case in point is one in which the plant manager asked his maintenance foreman why a particular job had not been taken care of. The foreman responded, "I don't know; I told Charlie once." (Charlie was the mechanic assigned to the job.) With this answer, the foreman displayed not only weakness in communication with his man but weak foremanship in his response to his superior.

There are two primary purposes of communication:

1. To provide the information and understanding necessary to individual or group effort. This can be done by training the workers in the techniques of the job. It can be called *the skill to work.*
2. To provide the attitudes necessary for motivation, cooperation, and job satisfaction. This can be called *the will to work.*

The formula, then, is *the skill to work + the will to work = the best work.*

Communication has a technical framework and an organizational framework. The *technical* framework is made up of signs or symbols. The *organizational* framework is the environment in which communication takes place.

The science of semantics deals with the relationships among communication symbols and with the meaning of words, and it is this meaning that must be communicated from one person to another. Unfortunately, the same word does not mean the same thing to all people. Life would be much easier if it did. The meaning placed upon a word is influenced by the individual differences of the human receiver, who may, in addition, choose one of several meanings which suits him best. It depends upon his particular experience and what he wants to make of it.

For example, the foreman's statement to his worker, "Get on that job as soon as you can," leaves the foreman wide open. He may assume that his employee will get to it within several hours, but the employee's experience indicates that nobody starts a new job after 3:30 P.M. even if there is little else to do. Furthermore, if it is an unpleasant job, the worker may not be too anxious to get to it at all. Here is a clear case of poor communication on the part of the foreman. The employee takes the words "as soon as you can" to mean the next day at the earliest (in terms of his experience) or later than that if possible (in terms of his attitude). The foreman is in error because he has (1) assumed that the employee knows what is meant; (2) assumed that he knows how the employee feels; and (3) assumed that the employee understands what he—the foreman —means.

In the simplest terms, two of the cardinal principles of communication are:

1. Don't make assumptions.
2. Address the receiver in terms of his experience and attitude.

The Job of Listening

Since meaning is communicated by the voice, listening is of special importance. Socrates said, "Nature has given us two ears and two eyes, but one tongue to the end that we should hear and see more than we speak." In China, they put it differently. "The listener reaps," says a Chinese proverb, "while the talker sows." Whatever way it is stated, listening is one of the most important secrets of successful foremanship.

Listening is not simply *hearing* what the other person says but also *understanding* what he says. It means thinking about what the speaker is saying, searching for what he may be unable to say, and even helping him, if necessary, to say what he means. The foreman cannot be thinking of what he is going to say as soon as the employee stops to take a breath. A tennis player cannot dictate his next shot; he must wait until the ball is returned to him.

Listening properly requires two ears, one for meaning and the other for feeling. The foreman must hear more than the words uttered. He must listen to the whole person, his background, and the way he responds to situations. Is he an optimist, a pessimist, or an alarmist? Such information forms the context for what he says, and when the foreman listens only to words, he is taking those words —which can mean almost anything—out of context.

These suggestions may help the foreman to do a better job of listening:

1. Listen to the other person—learn his past history, temperament, intelligence, and reaction habits.
2. Do not interrupt. Instead, encourage him to talk until the message he wishes to convey is clear.
3. Do not offer a hasty answer, especially if you are uncertain of the individual's meaning. Better ask questions for more information.
4. Do not anticipate or assume that the other person's meaning is obvious. He can sense this and either remain silent or go off on a tangent.
5. Listen until the employee's *actual* need is understood. The stenographer who complains about her typewriter may really want to know whether she is going to get one of the new ones on order.

No one remembers all he knows. The good foreman must listen to ideas rather than words as a conscious, positive act—not just expose himself to sound.

Language and Its Aids

It is language, of course, by way of the spoken and the written word, that has the widest use in management communication. But the listener's task is complicated by the fact that, aside from the interpretation which the speaker places upon words in terms of his experience and attitudes, the words themselves have a variety of meanings. For example, the simple term "round" may suggest something shaped like a cylinder or a ball; when used with the word "trip," it may mean a complete journey to a destination plus the return to the point of origin; and we also speak of "a round of beef" and a "round" that is sung. In fact, this one word "round" has 73 different meanings. To make his instructions clear, therefore, the foreman must be careful that the words he uses have the meaning for the receiver which he intended.

Pictures are frequently used in communication of all kinds. Greater, clearer, and longer lasting impressions are made upon the receiver when pictures are added to words, primarily because another sense, that of sight, is added to the sense of sound. Advertising has been one of the greatest users of pictures along with descriptive text, and television commercials have a much greater impact than the radio commercials of years ago. Many companies use films in job training, safety campaigns, and so on. Thus the foreman who can add charts, blueprints, layouts, or other visual aids to his words will improve communication.

Action is another important communication device for the foreman. His handshake, his smile, and his general bearing are full of meaning. Failure to act also communicates something. When the foreman is too busy to compliment a worker on a good job or to take a promised action, the message communicated to the employees may lead them to a conclusion which the foreman never anticipated.

In any action or lack of action, then, the foreman is constantly communicating with his people. From the very moment of his appointment as a foreman he starts to live in a glass house; it can safely be said that the eyes of at least one of his people are on him at all times. Many different interpretations are put upon his actions and behavior and passed along through the work group. In numerous cases, particularly in small communities, even the foreman's actions off the job are messages of one kind or another to his people. This is one of the elements of his job which makes it so difficult.

Organization and Communication

The organizational framework of communication, we have stated, provides the environment in which it takes place. Organizations give each person a certain job to perform. A helper in a garage has a quite different job from the garage foreman. Their functions are different, their interests are different, and their organizational level and social status are different. Whether or not these different factors are barriers to communication, we can say that they at least influence the way the two workers communicate.

The formal organization arises from delegated authority, responsibility, and procedure. It may be reduced to writing in the form of job descriptions and organization charts. Most management people prefer a formal organization because it can be controlled and is relatively easy to work with when it is understood and accepted.

However, there is also an informal organization which is unwritten and uncharted but must be dealt with. It grows out of the social interaction of people and thus is fickle, dynamic, and varied; its leadership may change quickly. But any group of people interested in their work will normally communicate with each other through the the informal device known as the "grapevine."

Many people in management—particularly foremen, who are closest to it—wish the grapevine did not exist and feel that it does exist and grow only because of some inattention on their part. More than one foreman has believed that the existence of an active grapevine was a mark against him. This, however, is not necessarily so. A grapevine will always flourish and, in fact, *should* flourish in an active group of concerned workers. It is not the existence of the grapevine (there will inevitably be one) but what the foreman does with it that matters.

Certainly, the grapevine has undesirable characteristics. It can spread rumors and untruths, it is not responsible for mistakes, and it is not easy to pin down. On the other hand, it has many desirable characteristics. It gives insight into employee attitudes and provides a safety valve for employee emotions. It can help to spread useful information, and, very importantly, it can help to translate management's more formal language into the more understandable language of the worker. It may even carry information which the formal system has omitted.

Living with the Grapevine

The grapevine obviously has a strong influence on communication, and the influence can be either favorable or unfavorable. The foreman should be realistic enough to accept it. Experience has proved that it cannot be suppressed or weeded out; it has to be lived with.

Recently, the grapevine in a New England company spread the rumor that all women employees would be "laid off next week." There was some basis for the rumor because the day before there had been a meeting of all production foremen. (Every time such a meeting takes place, the employees wonder what is going to happen next.) The foremen were told that the government contract on which the women employees were working would be canceled.

Almost before the meeting broke up, the grapevine was running faster than any of the production equipment. And, as usual, the messages were relayed so as to circumvent the foreman. Jobs were plentiful, and the labor market was tight; the result of this situation was that a number of trained women employees left for jobs with other companies before the rumor could be dispelled. What were the actual facts? It was true that the particular government contract in question had been canceled, but another one had been awarded to the company in its place, and no layoff had been planned by management.

Company after company suffers great losses every year because of similar misunderstandings. Not only are millions of man-days lost because employees do not have the facts and quit, but even more costly is the reduced efficiency of employees who remain on the job but are confused or bitter because of rumors they have heard.

Much can be done about harmful rumors and half-truths spread by the grapevine, and it is up to the foreman to do it. First, he should listen to what his employees really think, what they want to know, and how they feel about things. Here are some of the things that workers want to know (the foreman should make up his own checklist):

1. Background, organization, and general operations of the company. Its products—where and how they are made and where they go.

2. Company policies—particularly new policies and their effect.
3. Company plans for changes and how the workers will be affected.
4. Ways in which their jobs fit into the whole; how promotion may be gained.
5. Business outlook and prospects for steady work.
6. The company's income and its plans for future expansion or new products.
7. Information about layoffs if they should become necessary: advance notice, reasons why, ways in which they will be affected.

At this point, the foreman should follow up by telling his people the facts about policies, operations, economics, and other subjects on his checklist. Facts are the best remedy for rumors. By talking things over with his employees today, the foreman will be inoculating them against infection tomorrow by the germs of doubt, distrust, and suspicion. Furthermore, in so doing the foreman will be using the grapevine to his advantage. When he is talking to one individual, he is actually talking to many other employees.

Barriers to Communication

In the best formal organizations, there are theoretically clear channels of communication. Messages should flow rapidly and easily —but they don't. There are barriers in each direction that block communication. However, these barriers can be broken down or, at least, reduced if they are known and studied.

Some of the barriers to *downward* communication are these:

1. The tendency is for each party to make his own interpretations by altering the communication a little.
2. Selective interpretation occurs. Each person accepts and remembers only those parts of the message that he wishes to believe.
3. The method of communication fails. The message is not clearly stated.

4. The integrity of the management is distrusted. People distrust anything management says in a "negative" climate.
5. Employees have greater confidence in other sources of information, such as the grapevine.
6. The foreman himself is a hostile, cold, and indifferent person who gives the impression that all management is the same way.

Some barriers to *upward* communication are the following:

1. The "sunflower effect" prevails. This is the tendency of people to be overly concerned with impressing the boss and so pass on only that information which will make them look good.
2. The foreman has too much work and not enough time.
3. The foreman hears only what he wants to hear. (This is the ostrich act!)
4. There is a tendency to warp or distort a message in passing it on.
5. Workers distrust the superior, so they tell him nothing.

To improve downward communication, the following actions can be taken:

1. Phrase instructions in clear, simple, down-to-earth language. Remember that visual aids are also a means of communicating.
2. Supplement oral communication by written material—manuals, rules in writing, and so on.
3. Make all communication two-way. By means of the "feedback system," instructions should be repeated back and forth to make certain that they have been understood.

To improve upward communication, the foreman can do the following:

1. Become a good listener. This is part of the favorable communication climate.
2. Use the consultative approach with employees to help in

making the right decisions. This also contributes to creating a favorable climate.

3. Supplement the usual channels of communication with exit interviews, follow-up interviews, and a study of grievances.

If there is good communication, several situations will result:

1. There will be an understanding of each other's problems by top managers, supervisors, and employees.
2. There will be minimal barriers to communication, and material will be clearly, simply, and logically presented and thus understood.
3. Management will explain the reasons for its rules, regulations, and policies to aid in the employees' understanding and acceptance of them.
4. Management will show by its *deeds,* not just by its words, that it is interested in the employees' welfare.
5. Employees will be given ample opportunity to participate in the decisions which affect them.

There is no such thing as perfection in communication. There *are* varying degrees of skill; some people take to communication naturally while others muddle through. But, for most people, the problem is to bring skill to the point where it helps rather than impedes progress.

Generally, the path to increased effectiveness in any area lies in an impatience with the status quo. Aside from the changes which have to be made as, for example, shifts take place in the organization, it is important for the foreman to set continually higher goals —readier acceptance, faster response, and more information.

13

CONTROLLING TURNOVER

THE CONSCIENTIOUS FOREMAN who is concerned with doing his full job of cost control and cost reduction must be keenly interested in the movement of people into and out of his department. This movement is of two kinds—the shifting of employees within the company and the movement of people into and out of the company. To some degree, every department in the company is a self-contained unit for the foreman in charge, and both kinds of mobility present the same kinds of opportunities and dangers for him.

Within limits, when properly handled and controlled, both kinds of personnel movement can be good for the company and for the department foreman as well. It is when the movement of people is excessive that it becomes destructive of individual and organizational stability. This is particularly true of the movement of people into and out of the company, which is known as *turnover*.

When a member is lost, the work group must adjust in some fashion. Until a replacement is found, changes in schedule and assignments for others in the group are inevitable. If the departing employee was highly valued by his teammates and was discharged without adequate explanation, the balance of the group may become disturbed. Speculations leading to rumors and gossip frequently follow such a discharge and inevitably reduce work efficiency. This discharge may even shake the group to the point that it precipitates other quits which further upset the group.

When a new man is hired and introduced into the department, adjustments also must be made by all parties. While the new employee has the greatest adjustment to make (a good induction and a fully implemented orientation program will help), some effort must be exerted by all employees in the department. The old-timers may ask each other, "Who is this new guy? He doesn't look as though he would fit in." And the "new guy," confronted with what may seem to be a clique, can become discouraged to the point of quitting at the end of the first or second day.

The adjustments by which the entire group adapts to a new member and the new employee becomes a part of the group are often difficult. If not carefully handled by an alert foreman, the strain may show up in production—increased spoilage, reduced output, accidents, or arguments. If the adjustment process is not completed satisfactorily, the entire replacement cycle will have to start over again with a new man.

Turnover Costs

The movement of personnel into and out of the company obviously involves costs which, unless balanced by some gain, represent a loss. The actual dollar amount of the loss varies, according to surveys made, from a low figure of a hundred to many thousands of dollars per man. Some of the elements involved are so intangible that an accurate dollar cost cannot be placed upon them. Yet line foremen are frequently unaware of the cost of excessively high turnover rates.

In order to reduce the cost of turnover, it is essential that the foreman be aware of all of the separate costs involved. They are:

1. The cost of hiring and training a new employee (the greater the skill of the departed employee and the sooner he leaves after his training is completed, the greater the loss to the company).
   a. Employment costs—recruiting, interviewing, physical examinations, records, and so on.

    b. Training costs—time of foreman or other employee.

    c. Pay to the trainee (beyond what he produces)—especially if there is a guaranteed minimum, not really earned at the outset.

    d. Increased scrap and waste of materials while trainee is learning.

    e. Possible cost of accidents during learning.

2. The cost of overtime required from regular workers who must maintain production until the new employee is fully trained.

3. The loss of production between the time when one employee leaves and the time when his replacement reaches full productivity. (It is high until the replacement is found; then it decreases slowly during the adjustment period.)

4. The loss in partly idle equipment during the training period.

All these costs and losses are always present in turnover, but they are difficult to compute because each element varies in degree. It is obvious that the total cost is higher in a tight labor market when jobs are plentiful and people are more difficult to find. It should be equally obvious that the most unjustifiable extravagance is the loss involved in "avoidable" separations. These are the ones that the foreman should be most concerned with, and they are frequently concealed in a single, overall turnover figure. The only way to ferret out and distinguish between avoidable and unavoidable separations is careful analysis of the current rate of turnover in the department.

How Turnover Is Computed

Turnover is commonly expressed in two rates—one for separations and the other for accessions (new hires). In this chapter, only the separation rate will be considered.

Separations or terminations of employment are usually subdivided as follows:

1. *Quit*—separation initiated by the worker. Workers who are absent without authorization or notification for a stipulated number of days are usually classified as quits.

2. *Layoff*—termination of employment by the company because a job is being eliminated or the workforce is being reduced. (A general shutdown of a department for inventory or mechanical repairs, or the suspension of an employee as a form of punishment, should not be classified as a layoff.)
3. *Discharge*—termination initiated by the employer because he is dissatisfied with the employee's performance or behavior. It follows that this separation is prejudicial to the employee's record.

It is important that the foreman understand these designations, particularly when he is interviewing candidates for employment. It is not unusual for an applicant to write "laid off" under "reason for leaving" a prior job when, in fact, he was discharged. He may not know the difference, or he may falsify the record deliberately because being laid off looks better. A check with the prior employer will usually reveal the true situation.

The U.S. Department of Labor's Bureau of Labor Statistics uses the following method for computing the separation rate:

1. Determine the average number of employees for a given period (usually a calendar month) by adding together the number of employees on the payroll at the beginning and at the end of the period. Then divide the sum by two.
2. Divide the total number of separations during the period by the average employment figure arrived at in Step 1.
3. Multiply the number by 100 to get the rate, as a percentage, for the period.

Reduced to a formula, the equation is

$$\frac{Total\ Separations\ for\ Period}{Average\ Number\ on\ Payroll\ for\ Period} \times 100 = \frac{Separation\ Rate}{(percent)}$$

For example, a department had 24 employees at the beginning of a month and 26 employees at the end of the same month. When added together and divided by 2, these figures indicate an average for the month of 25. The total number of separations for the month is 5.

$$\frac{5}{25} \times 100 = 20\ percent$$

An annual rate may be obtained by multiplying the actual monthly rate by a factor equal to 365 divided by the number of days in the given month. Unless this is done, the monthly figures are not quite comparable to the annual rate because of the varying number of days in the months. To carry the example just given to an annual rate, if the 20 percent figure were for the month of February in a leap year with 29 days;

$$\frac{365}{29} \times 20 \text{ percent} = 252 \text{ percent}$$

This would mean that the entire department would turn over a bit more than two and one-half times (about 63 people) to maintain a constant average workforce of 25. At a computed cost of $400 per separation, the total annual cost of turnover would be $25,200, an excessive amount for any foreman. If this foreman could reduce his turnover to a more normal figure of 4 percent per month, or about 50 percent for the year (13 people), at the same estimated cost of $400 per separation, he could reduce his yearly departmental losses by $20,000.

However, the turnover figure for a department or a company by itself is almost meaningless. It must be compared with some standard such as industry as a whole or other companies in a particular industry. The Bureau of Labor Statistics publishes such comparative figures each month in its *Monthly Labor Review*. These data are obtained from many thousands of representative companies in more than one hundred different industries. The foreman should watch these published figures and measure his own department's rates against them.

But, even if the departmental figures compare favorably with others, the foreman should not be satisfied unless he is sure that the rate of voluntary separations is as low as possible and until he has learned all he can from the figures as to how effective he is in handling his personnel.

Why Are They Leaving?

The first question the foreman should ask himself is, "Why are employees voluntarily leaving my department?" Is it because they think they can find a better job somewhere else? If so, why does the new job look better? Are people dissatisfied with the pay, with the working conditions, with the foreman, with other employees, with work assignments? Or are they leaving because of illness, family pressure, school matriculation, marriage, pregnancy, or other personal reasons?

Frequently the foreman does not know why an employee leaves when he goes of his own accord. Usually the departing worker will give some reason to the foreman when he gives notice, but often this reason is not the real one. The employee may not know the real reason or, more likely, does not care to reveal it. He frequently resorts to "ill health" or "needed at home" as his reasons for leaving because these are difficult to disprove. However, there are ways to determine his real reason, and someone in the company should make the effort.

The exit interview, held when the employee leaves or calls back for his final pay check, may bring out the real reason, but even then the employee may not feel that he can talk freely—particularly if he is interviewed by his foreman, who may be a part of the reason. In most cases the exit interview is best conducted by someone other than the immediate foreman; the personnel office can do it effectively; however, in the absence of a centralized personnel function, an office manager or controller can do as well. In any event, the following steps will serve as a guide to the conduct of an exit interview:

1. A preliminary investigation of the employee's record should be made by the interviewer prior to the exit interview. This information should be reviewed:
   a. Service, age, marital status, previous experience, education, and other pertinent factors.
   b. Nature of present job, hours of work, shift, rate of pay, medical record, attendance record, foreman's opinion of the employee, and other work-related data.
   c. The employee's stated reason for leaving. This information should be obtained directly from the employee's foreman.
2. In conducting the interview itself, the interviewer should follow these instructions:
   a. Interview under conditions of maximum privacy.

    b. Make a brief statement regarding the company's interest in retaining the employee's services and the employee's possible interest in retaining the benefits accumulated under various company plans and policies. The employee may wish to reconsider employment at some future date.

    c. Allow the employee to tell his story, giving the reason or reasons for leaving in detail.

    d. Answer questions he may have and clear up any misunderstanding. If questions are complex, consult with others to obtain satisfactory answers.

    e. Do not make commitments that cannot be fulfilled. If the employee decides at this late date that he would like to continue his employment or wishes to reconsider, follow through with his foreman and any others involved until the case can be considered closed.

    f. End the interview on friendly terms. The chief gain from it may be that it represents a friendly gesture from management.

3. Make a record of the interview on a form like the suggested exit interview chart in Exhibit 16. Periodic summaries of exit interviews should also be made to analyze the overall status of voluntary terminations.

Who Is Leaving?

In addition to information provided by the departing employees, something may be learned about the possible reasons behind voluntary separations if the foreman will ask himself a second question: "Where are these voluntary separations coming from?" He must know just what sections of his department employees are voluntarily leaving. What kind of work were they doing? Under what conditions? In any department (other than an assembly line) in which small groups work on special jobs under a lead man, the fault may be in the composition of the work group, in its teamwork, or in the lead man.

The answers to a third question, "What kind of employee is leaving voluntarily?" often provide further insight into the reasons

Exhibit 16

Suggested Exit Interview Chart

Employee's Name _____Date _____

Department _____Service ____ Years ____ Months ____

Foreman _____Job Title _____ Wage _____

GENERAL INFORMATION:

When did you decide to quit? Suddenly? _____ Some time ago? _____

Why? _____ ____

Would you consider working here if a change were made in wages? ____

Working conditions? _____ Supervision? _____ Other_____

WORKING RELATIONS:

1. How did you get along with the foreman? Very well _____ O.K. _____

   Not very well _____

2. Did the foreman ask for suggestions? Often _____ Rarely _____

3. Did the foreman keep you informed? Often _____ Rarely _____

4. Did the foreman handle your grievances promptly? Always _____

   Occasionally _____ Never _____

5. How did you get along with other workers? Very well ____ O.K. ____

   Not so well _____ Why? _____

WORKING CONDITIONS:

1. Did you think you should have received: More training? _____

   Less training? _____

2. Were you satisfied with your wages? Yes _____ No _____

3. How are working conditions here as compared with other plants?

   Better _____ About the same _____ Not so good _____

4. Would you advise your friends to work here? Yes _____ No _____

5. What kind of attitude do you think management has toward workers?

   Friendly _____ Unfriendly _____ Fair _____ Other _____

INTERVIEWER'S SUMMARY:

Worker's main criticism: _____

Interviewer's recommendations: _____

for quits. The age, sex, marital status, length of service, and skill of the worker who leaves voluntarily often fall into patterns that are worthy of study. If voluntary separations occur chiefly among very young workers of both sexes, among girls who are getting married, or among workers of less than three months' service, there may be less concern than when experienced, highly skilled employees are quitting. Nevertheless, the pattern which emerges may well provide the means of reducing voluntary separations.

Could a better indoctrination or induction program retain more employees beyond the three-month point? What is being done to make young employees feel that their youth is an asset to the company? What educational opportunities are being offered in the company to stimulate employees toward self-development? Are the employees given an opportunity to participate in planning and decision making and to advance themselves? These and many other questions should be asked.

Unless a careful record is kept of separations, it is impossible to determine where they are occurring and what kind of employees are leaving voluntarily. A termination record (see Exhibit 17) should be designed and used throughout the company; if none is required, the foreman should keep his own figures for analysis. The blank back of the form may be used for other data.

Maintaining Overall Stability

In addition to the specific steps the foreman must take to analyze and reduce labor turnover in his department, he is generally responsible for maintaining labor stability in his department. He should—

1. Take a personal interest in his employees. (This does not mean fraternizing.) Demonstrate this interest by seeing that each person receives all the benefits that are coming to him. Study individuals in terms of their qualifications and peculiarities to avoid misfits.
2. Develop good workers. Be particular about training new people and getting them started right. New employees are the ones most likely to become dissatisfied—they may

Exhibit 17

Termination Record

Department _____   Period _____ to _____

Classification	Sex	Hired	Re-employed	TERMINATIONS					Avge. No. in Force	Turnover Rate		Length of Service			
				Dis-charged	Laid Off	Re-signed	Other Causes	Total		This Mo. %	Last Mo. %	Less than 3 months	3 mos. to 1 yr.	1 to 5 yrs.	Over 5 yrs.
	M														
	F														
	M														
	F														
	M														
	F														
	M														
	F														
	M														
	F														
	M														
	F														
	M														
	F														
Recapitulation:	M														
	F														
Total															

leave within the first several months. Older employees should be developed for better and more responsible jobs so that they can be advanced when the opportunity presents itself. These employees often leave if they become convinced that there is no future for them.

3. Provide good working conditions. A foreman has considerable control over safety and sanitation in his department. Proper ventilation and lighting not only help to increase production but reduce job dissatisfactions. Discourage cliques and encourage a friendly climate. If conditions outside the department are causing dissatisfaction, explain this to the employees and let management know.

4. Be firm but fair with everyone. Do not show favoritism.

5. Know what an employee has to do to be considered for promotion and let him know.

6. Review the earnings of individual employees. If the basic rate structure needs adjustment, let management know.

7. Adjust complaints and grievances as quickly as possible. Clear up misunderstandings; feed facts to the grapevine to stem false rumors.

8. Present management policies and departmental rules in an understandable way. Most rules exist to serve the employee's best interests as well as the company's.

9. Avoid unnecessary layoffs. When they *are* necessary, assist in arranging for transfers or jobs elsewhere in the community.

10. See that an employee does not leave voluntarily before his real reason is determined. The foreman should report the stated reason to the exit interviewer.

11. Make every effort to solve the problems revealed by studies of exit interviews and termination records.

12. Develop leadership. Employees respect and stay with a foreman who they feel is looking out for them. Most people are loyal to a person or any situation to the degree that it it seems to serve their best interests.

❋ ❋ ❋

In conclusion, it must be said that turnover is not all bad. A reasonable amount must exist to promote organizational stability by bringing in new blood. Internal mobility within a department or between departments may help individuals, improve teamwork, and raise morale. But both kinds of mobility require adjustments by the people involved. Turnover adjustments cost money. In order to determine whether the cost is balanced by the gains, the foreman needs to know what the exact cost is, why his employees are leaving, where the voluntary separations are coming from, and what kind of employee is leaving. The only way to improve the situation is through constant study.

14

DEVELOPING UNDERSTUDIES

In sports, especially professional baseball, "depth of the bench" has always been an all-important factor in the position of a team in its league at the end of the season. A ball club these days consists of 25 players, yet only 9 are on the field at any one time in a ball game; the other 16 sit on the bench. However, "depth of the bench" has little to do with the *number* of reserve players; rather, it means the *caliber* and *versatility* of the players—their ability to play one or more positions as well as the team members in the field. The team on the bench has decided the outcome of many ball games.

The same is true in the military and in business. In times of international crisis, the number and caliber of reserve officers and enlisted men will often help to prevent a real outbreak of war. If war does begin, the reserves will help to win the struggle. In business, trained personnel who are to take over key positions when necessary make the difference between sustained advancement and stumbling progress or outright failure. Most business organizations today recognize that they are much more competitive by virtue of their management team than they are by virtue of their products. Why? Because many products currently on the market are so similar that the consumer cannot detect the difference. But the company with the team that can produce and market its products most efficiently and effectively will usually lead the field.

The Need for Understudies

One of top management's high-priority duties should be to see that, whatever happens, there is always someone to carry on in each responsible job. The only way that an organization can perpetuate itself without going outside the company to fill vacancies is to develop understudies. Under this policy, the foreman is expected to safeguard all key jobs in his department, especially his own, with one or more trained men to fill them upon demand.

While many companies have an active policy of training understudies at all levels, some companies allow this policy to become weak or nonexistent at the foreman level, and still others have no such policy operating at any level. In such situations, the foreman must take it upon himself to develop at least an understudy for his own job. The presence of an understudy in his organization, even if it is only a small department, is an indication of good foremanship.

Why is this so essential? The foreman should not be fooled by the old adage, "If you want a thing done right, do it yourself." No foreman can function effectively in this way, and the foreman who tries it generally invites failure: He does nothing well, or favors one function to the neglect of another equally important one, or keeps himself from being promoted because he has no one trained to take his place. More than one man has unknowingly lost a promotional opportunity (and never known why) because he had no one to fill his job.

There is a physical limit to what the foreman can do. He must intelligently delegate work and authority to others to assure himself and the company of most effective results when he is present and a minimum of disturbance and delay when he is not.

Of course, there are difficulties involved in developing understudies. Nothing worthwhile is ever gained by an easy route. Once the foreman is convinced that an understudy is essential to his own performance and advancement, he will find the time to provide capable substitutes for every key job in his department.

There are many reasons why some foremen (and top managers, too) are reluctant to train an understudy. An understudy requires delegation, and a foreman may not admit that he does not want to delegate or doesn't know how to. He often rationalizes with such statements as "The nature of the job doesn't permit it"; "My subordinates are incompetent"; "My boss won't let me delegate"; or "There is too much work to delegate." There is usually no basis in fact for any of these statements. The foreman often is simply afraid he may end up without any job—although no foreman ever delegated himself out of a job unless it was into a better one. The most ineffectual way for any man to try to insure his security in his job is to withhold information about it from his subordinates.

Another bit of weak reasoning on the part of a foreman is the belief that a trained understudy may be promoted to a better job in some other department. True, this works some inconvenience on the foreman. But the worst (or best) that could happen would be that top management looked to his department each time that it needed a good man to promote within the company. And, however difficult this might be for him, he would probably be looked upon as the best foreman in the company. His superiors would see him as a man who can work with and develop people—one of the most important skills a manager needs for top-level positions. Also, there would be a mad scramble among the better employees of the company to get into this foreman's department to take advantage of the advancement possibilities. Of course, he would lose a good man occasionally, but what a team of employees he would have!

No foreman can hope for greater success than a reputation for making other men successful. The foreman who helps an ambitious man prepare himself for bigger things is not only doing the best possible job for the man and the company but is, at the same time, broadening himself, increasing his value to the company, and improving his own efficiency.

The Advantages of an Understudy

There are many advantages to training and developing an understudy. The worker's desire to progress, a commendable trait in any individual, is satisfied. His present job becomes more secure as he aquires more knowledge and a greater sense of responsibility. The additional training and experience make him eligible for promotion and increased earnings. He becomes more interested in his work, has greater opportunity to use initiative, gains confidence, self-reliance, and prestige. He develops ingenuity, tact, patience, and ability; his morale and enthusiasm improve. In general, the training which an understudy experiences provides the medium through which his latent abilities come to the fore.

With one or more reliable, competent understudies, the foreman makes himself more valuable to his company and becomes more eligible for promotion. His work is easier, and he can accomplish more—including the pursuit of the information he needs to qualify for a higher position. In other words, he can now become an understudy to his own superior.

With a capable understudy, the foreman is relieved of anxiety if he becomes ill, attends meetings, or takes a vacation. He has a better chance to plan and study his job, gains satisfaction from helping others advance, and has the benefit of helpful ideas from his understudy.

The company also benefits from the development of an understudy. Tie-ups, delays, and spoilage due to the absence, resignation, transfer, or promotion of the foreman are prevented. The understudy builds morale, acts as a check on turnover, and avoids the need for outside recruiting. Greater efficiency and job pride are the rule. A company with a broad program of developing understudies from top to bottom usually has a preferred standing in the community as a good place in which to work.

It should be clear, then, that all parties gain: the understudy, the foreman, and the company. And the benefits are so great that the money and time devoted to this activity should be looked upon as an investment with a payoff of more than 100 percent in dividends.

Selecting an Understudy

The first step in developing an understudy is to select the proper man. Careful observation and formal or informal ratings by the foreman are necessary to preliminary selection.

A potential foreman understudy should have the qualities of leadership, high-grade workmanship, patience, and loyalty for the long pull. These are very general but necessary attributes. The foreman, however, cannot wait for such a paragon to appear in fully developed form. He must be able to see the signs of these traits and qualities in a host of little things from day to day. Some evidence of potential foremanship ability should be indicated by the answers to these questions.

1. Does the man master those jobs which are given him?
2. Does he have a high standard of workmanship?
3. Is his ability respected by others?
4. Does he get along well with his fellow workers?
5. Is there any indication that other men regard him as a leader—on or off the job?
6. Are his personal habits and appearance good?
7. Does he use his time to the best advantage?
8. Does he want to learn new things and understand them thoroughly? Is he studying at night school or by correspondence?
9. How well does he express himself? How well does he listen?
10. Does he seem to be a patient individual even when things go wrong?
11. Does he accept his responsibilities well?
12. Does he help others willingly when asked?
13. Does he instruct a new worker efficiently and make him feel at home?
14. Can he deal effectively with his superiors, presenting his ideas with desirable forcefulness yet being a good sport when his idea is not accepted?

No foreman could give any of his people a 100 percent score on these points, but 100 percent is not what is expected. If these points are made known to potential understudies, they will have targets to shoot at.

It may well be that an occasional individual will turn down an opportunity to train as an understudy when he becomes aware of the traits and qualities sought. Even though a man may rate very high on all 14 points, he should be alerted to two major decisions which he must make if he aspires to foremanship.

1. He must decide that his future now lies with management and no longer with the ranks. This is a decision which he must make once and for all if he hopes to progress to still

higher jobs in management. Also, he must realize that getting other people to do things is quite different from doing them himself—and not any easier. The foreman's job may *look* easier, but it is not.

2. He must decide whether he can "live in a glass house" without feeling restricted. A foreman is being judged by his people in terms of his behavior and the example he sets on the job and, in many cases, off the job as well.

All told, this is quite a large bill to fill. A few men find it too formidable and withdraw. However, American business is blessed with great numbers of men who want to progress, know what it takes, and find their jobs challenging.

In order to remove some of the guesswork from the selection of a potential understudy, the proper use of certain approved tests is frequently helpful. A personnel department will often arrange to give them. Although they should never be the sole screening device, they add to the total information on a candidate. They measure characteristics which are held to be important in any supervisory position and which only scientifically devised means can determine with any degree of accuracy. Among these characteristics are:

- *Intelligence*—the capacity to learn new things and the capacity to adjust readily to new situations.
- *Leadership*—including extroversion, dominance, self-confidence, and social independence. The candidate with a high degree of social dependence and a relatively low degree of extroversion, dominance, and self-confidence is likely to be a "soft" personality, indecisive and reluctant to make a decision if it means that he may be disliked by those affected.
- *Sales motivation*—meaning, in this connection, persuasiveness. Although most foremen have nothing to do with the sales function, they must be persuasive people who can sell ideas.
- *Detail skills*—in arithmetic, spelling, vocabulary, copying, checking, and the like. The tests reveal not only the degree to which a person uses his intelligence but also his ability to plan—which is, of course, a detail skill.
- *Supervisory skills*—particularly in the human relations area.

Standard tests reveal the degree of proficiency or knowledge in this aspect of the foreman's job. No untrained person should be ruled out because of a low score on such a test, but the results open up obvious areas for quick training.

In addition to tests, there are other important elements to be considered in selecting a man. Among the most important is his work record, which should be in his personnel file in the form of periodic evaluations (see Chapter 5). His evaluations should indicate that his total fitness has been "above average" with a plus in the areas of cooperation and dependability consistently for the past several years. He may have worked for other foremen in the past, and their evaluations should be considered.

In all, then there are at least three methods by which the candidate should be reviewed. There are the 14 questions which bear on the general qualities of the candidate, the battery of tests, and the summation of the performance evaluations of the man. It is suggested that the score on each of the three count for one-third of the total of 90 points (each segment has a full score of 30 points). It might be well, then to set a minimum total score of 70 points to be eligible. In such an arrangement no single segment should be scored at less than 20 points if a man is to be considered at all.

Length of service with the company or in the department will have some bearing on the choice but should not be controlling. In cases where two or more candidates have the same total score, the candidate with the greater seniority should be selected.

Training the Understudy

After the potential understudy has been selected, his development becomes important. One method often used is to let the trainee act as a working assistant—for example, breaking in a new employee or helping as needed during a rush period. Or he can be rotated through various jobs and given different responsibilities to see how he reacts when he is assigned duties which are not a part of his regular job.

The foreman must personally coach the understudy trainee and constantly supervise his work. Periodic short talks and questions are part of this process. Group meetings, at which principles and policies of management are discussed, allow trainees to share information and stimulate action. Trainees for foremanship are always interested in problems related to the handling of employees and in company policies.

Almost every understudy in training should avail himself of the opportunities provided by night schools and colleges. Thousands of ambitious men are taking advantage of these opportunities out of their own pockets and on their own time. If the work hours interfere, there are many accredited home study schools offering excellent courses for the man who wants to prepare himself for a management position. The degree of a man's activity in self-development is an excellent measure of his interest in his own progress. He must be sold on the truth of the saying that "what a man does when he doesn't have to do it largely determines what he will be when he can no longer help it." The capital investment he makes in money and effort benefits him just as capital investment in a home or business improvement offsets obsolescence and decreased market value.

It is assumed, of course, that the trainee subscribes to trade journals and papers or, at least, reads them as they are circulated systematically throughout the company. Furthermore, he should read not only publications directly connected with his particular industry but books and publications in the broad areas of labor relations, personnel, and general management.

A favorable climate for growth is a necessary prerequisite for the development of any living thing. Most men sincerely want to improve, and a free and friendly climate helps. Therefore, it is important that the foreman show the trainee that he is trusted, relied upon, and needed. The foreman should do everything he can to build self-respect and self-confidence in the trainee, who should enjoy four freedoms—the freedom to direct his own work, to try out new ideas, to speak and think independently, and to make his own mistakes and profit by them. No man can grow if he is being coddled or over-protected. The foreman should expect a lot from the understudy trainee, but not more than he can deliver.

Virtually every foreman will agree that the major part of his own competence has resulted from on-the-job experience under the guidance and coaching of his superior. He may also agree that he acquired some of his present ability by exposure to many experiences not directly connected with his day-to-day job. In other words, most foremen and even top managers have reached their present level of competence by being given exposure to real situations with the aid of their immediate superiors or other members of management.

So, in his turn, the foreman develops his understudy through everyday association with him. Every meeting he has with the man is an opportunity. And the most important daily lesson is the example the foreman sets. This lesson goes on every day, and no foreman can stop it. Personal example can boost or supplement other developmental activities, or it can negate or counteract their effect. The foreman who is conscious of its tremendous effect will be careful to set a good example himself and will do all in his power to see that other members of management set a good example insofar as his people are concerned.

The foreman should carefully evaluate the understudy's performance as an understudy. In his normal supervision of the man's work, he should observe particularly those areas in which the man needs help. These informal evaluations should not be careless, prejudiced, subjective, or incomplete. They should have three basic purposes:

1. To determine how the understudy is doing in terms of what is required of him on his present job.
2. To inventory his abilities in terms of advancement to the bigger job.
3. To indicate the understudy's strong points and weak areas; in other words, show where he needs help in order to win promotion.

Every evaluation should be followed by a counseling session between the foreman and the understudy. Both his strengths and his weaknesses should be discussed. This provides the greatest possible opportunity for the foreman to show his man that he considers his personal plans and needs of true importance and is making a concerted effort to help him grow.

15

FOREMAN AND UNION

A BOOK ON FOREMANSHIP would be remiss if it did not consider the problem of unionism. The economic and political strength of unions has grown since the New Deal of the 1930's and has continued to have a tremendous influence on the attitudes, philosophies, and economic conditions of the American worker. This could not have happened without a continuing reappraisal of the personnel function and of company policies, with particular emphasis upon the foreman and his role.

Historical Background

World War I produced a labor shortage which, in turn, brought on what was probably the first recognition of the need for improved hiring policies and practices. In an effort to meet this need, what is now known as the personnel function got its start. Unionism was launched in earnest at this time, and by 1920 some 5 million workers had been organized.

Membership dropped during the next decade, probably owing to the increased adoption of industrial personnel programs. Indeed, one of the primary purposes of early personnel programs was to weaken the growth of unionism. Many of the personnel activities were paternalistic in nature, designed to look after the employees' welfare; in fact, the person in charge was often called the manager of employee welfare. At the same time, unions had little or no support from the government or the courts.

The Great Depression of the 1930's, with upward of 14 million workers unemployed, brought about a resurgence of unionism, and management took a new look at its own social responsibilities. The right of workers to organize and bargain collectively with their employers became law with the passage of the National Labor Relations (Wagner) Act of 1935. This was amended in 1947 by the Labor Management Relations (Taft-Hartley) Act and again in 1957. Today union membership numbers approximately 17 million workers.

Back in the 1920's, when "employee welfare" programs were increasing, the action taken by management was unilateral. Employee golf courses and swimming pools were built solely to "do good" for the employees. Company managements often became quite bitter when their employees joined unions and even struck after these welfare programs had been established and millions of dollars spent.

In the late thirties, one large company in the New York metropolitan area was suffering a prolonged strike. A passerby had the following conversation with one of the pickets:

"What is the cause of your strike?"
"We have organized a union, and we want recognition."
"I have always heard that X Company was good to its employees. Only a few months ago, it built them a swimming pool."
"That's right, but nobody ever asked us whether we wanted a swimming pool."

In other words, the employees resented such unilateral action; they wanted the company to recognize that they had an organization which would represent their interests and so replace unilateral with bilateral action. They succeeded.

With the government's protection, unions today derive their strength from striving to help the workers in all types of organizations to fulfill certain basic needs and to achieve certain goals which are important to them.

Workers Want Unions

The chapter on motivation has explained which goals and needs are most important at any given time to the man at work. Much depends upon the extent to which the worker has already satisfied his needs. While good wages, job security, and promotional opportunities are valued highly by most workers, so are the respect of other workers, fair treatment by the foreman and the company, and participation in decisions that affect them. For example, unions have increased their membership by using their bargaining power to win higher wages, shorter hours, and a greater degree of security for their members, but many workers have joined unions only to satisfy some long-held grievance against the foreman in the shop or against the company as a whole.

The natural, but ever-increasing, desire of the workers to have a greater "say" in the decisions that affect them may be more democratic, but it undoubtedly makes the job of the foreman more difficult. The foreman today must have more intelligence, leadership skill, and understanding than ever before. He must know how to keep his "house in order," whether or not there is a union, and he must know what to do or not do during an organizing effort. A third responsibility—knowing how to operate under a collective agreement when there is one—deserves a chapter in itself.

The question often arises as to whether workers would desire unions if management policies had always been sound and the workers had been given a greater opportunity to participate in the decisions which affect them. Some companies have felt that unions could be eliminated or reduced in importance by good programs. It appears that workers still require unions to preserve what they already enjoy. If the company expands its personnel program on the assumption that workers will find unionization unnecessary or less desirable, it is making the wrong assumption. This is not to say that a company should not expand its personnel program; however, the company should not be disappointed or feel that it has been "stabbed in the back" if the employees still organize. No company should strive to prevent unionization at all costs. The growth of the labor movement and the presence of a union in a plant should serve to make good foremen better foremen.

Putting the House in Order

There are many steps which a management should take to put its house in order. In most cases, management must rely upon its foremen to see that these steps are taken. Certainly, they constitute no guarantee against a union, but to the degree that they have been taken, it can be safely said that the relationship with the union will probably be less militant, more intelligent, and much more comfortable.

Putting the house in order, either before a union organizing effort or after a union is firmly established, calls for—

1. Comparing wages and fringe benefits with area and industry practices, making necessary adjustments where practicable.
2. Informing foremen so that they, in turn, can instruct employees on any and all changes or developments affecting their jobs and the company.
3. Checking on employees with a record of substandard performance. Union contract seniority provisions can restrict disciplinary action later.
4. Adhering to good hiring procedures for all people. Do not discriminate—check thoroughly.
5. Making certain, if employment is part time, temporary, or seasonal, that the employee understands this when hired.
6. Broadening the employment base as much as possible in terms of age, race, and other factors.
7. Acquainting new employees with their duties and obligations, as well as company benefits and advantages.
8. Making sure that company, plant, and department rules are clearly written out, thoroughly explained, and equitably and consistently enforced.
9. Making sure that practices are uniform from department to department.
10. Disposing of all complaints, even those that are seemingly minor or unimportant, quickly and fairly. Preferably, this should be a job for the foreman.

What else should a company foreman do? He should—

1. Be sure that all complaints and grievances, with their disposition, are reported to top management. They should be reviewed periodically for patterns of type and effective adjustment.
2. Have a uniform system for handling complaints and grievances.
3. Maintain complete, accurate, and up-to-date records of all complaints and grievances and their disposition.
4. Assist management in keeping lines of communication open.
5. Set reasonable standards of employee performance and inform employees of what is expected.
6. Review the performance of his employees periodically and point the way to improvement. Commend those employees who do well and maintain records of ratings and reviews.
7. Inform his people of lines of promotion within or outside the department and outline the qualifications for higher jobs. The policy of promotion from within should be adhered to wherever possible.
8. Lay off workers according to skill, ability, and length of service in the department, plant, or company; never play favorites.
9. Have an organization chart available for reference so that each person knows his area of responsibility and authority.
10. Have job descriptions which show functions, duties, responsibilities, and relationships for each job. Compensation can then be graduated and related to each job according to a structure that is readily understood by the employees. (This, of course, is not the responsibility of the individual foreman.)
11. Maintain accurate, complete, and up-to-date records available for wage-hour and equal employment opportunities commission inspection.
12. Avoid such entanglements as the intermingling of nonunion employees with unionized groups.
13. Arrange for personal counseling when desired by employees.

14. Recognize and appreciate the foreman's role as company representative, especially in employee relations.
15. Arrange an exit interview for any employee quitting his job.

It should be obvious from this list that one of three conditions can exist in a company that does not have a union:

1. Very few of the suggested steps have been taken or even contemplated.
2. A partial start has been made, and perhaps one-third to one-half of the proposals are under way and working well; but because the parties concerned are all busy, the program has never been completed. It was set aside "temporarily," but that happened so long ago that it would be difficult to pick it up now and proceed further. Nothing more has been done, and even that portion that was working well has degenerated somewhat because of weakened interest and lack of follow-up.
3. All the suggestions have been vigorously carried out for a period of time. But, because of personnel changes, a new top management with a different viewpoint, and no union effort to organize the workers, interest has waned.

If any of the three conditions exist in his department, the foreman should take the initiative, through his meetings with management, to see that more attention is given to putting the house in order. If there is some step in the list which he can take by himself, he should do so without waiting for it to be adopted as company policy. In any case, programs in the personnel field should not only be viable but flexible. They should be checked periodically for effectiveness. Changes, modifications, or additions may have to be made to meet changing conditions. In other words, there is nothing static about this important work.

The foreman must constantly check and recheck the personnel function as it operates in his department when a union gains recognition and the first labor-management agreement is completed. Some unions will insist on a "zipper clause," which, in effect, provides that any privilege enjoyed by the employees at the time that the union is recognized must be continued for the life of the contract. Such a provision holds whether the privilege is specifically mentioned in the the contract or company rules or not. It may be a privilege informally granted by one foreman just to be nice to his people. Some examples are:

- Extended coffee breaks or coffee breaks in addition to a stipulated rest period.
- A job paying a special premium or a rate higher than what the agreement calls for.
- An early quitting time to allow the employees to wash up and leave the plant by the specified quitting time.

These and many other such privileges should not be granted hastily by the foreman. Arbitrators usually hold that such practices must be continued, depending upon their frequency and pervasiveness.

During the Organizing Drive

The next major area for the consideration of all managers and foremen, individually and collectively, opens up when a union begins an organizing effort. The laws and the rulings of the National Labor Relations Board and the courts have been such as to push the "caution" button for management during this period. The following actions should be taken:

1. Maintain plant and departmental discipline; foremen should not be frightened into permitting conduct which would not be tolerated under normal circumstances. Keep accurate records to support any action taken.
2. Do not discriminate between union sympathizers and nonunion workers in such matters as work assignments, overtime, vacation schedules, or wage increases.
3. Adopt the rule that "working time is for work." Do not, however, make any company rules which restrict union activities during rest periods, lunch periods, or before and after work.
4. If two or more unions are competing against each other, do

not grant privileges to one union which are denied to the other.

5. Do not prohibit employees from wearing union buttons or union insignia on their street clothing or personal property. Keep union slogans, insignia, and literature off company bulletin boards, furniture, and equipment.

6. Tell the company's side of the story to the employees in a positive manner. Detail the benefits they have been given and are presently receiving. Do not debate union charges or make countercharges since this gives the union more material for discussion.

7. Conduct business in a normal manner. Do not change past practices with regard to wage increases, work assignments, or hiring just because a union organizing effort is in progress.

8. Do not ignore existing complaints or defer their settlement.

9. Do not make any promises to employees in order to influence them against the union. Likewise, do not threaten employees because of their pro-union sympathies.

10. Do not question employees about their union sympathies unless the only intention is to find out whether the union represents the majority of the employees. Questioning in bad faith is an unfair labor practice.

11. Do not initiate or assist in the preparation of anti-union petitions or employee anti-union activities.

12. Avoid unfair labor practices; they can result in delaying a representation election or in setting it aside.

13. Keep a record of all union activities. Do not, however, engage in spying or surveillance merely to obtain and keep such a record.

14. If the union approaches either company customers or suppliers and asks them to stop doing business with the company, file secondary boycott charges with the National Labor Relations Board.

15. If the union pickets the company premises without petitioning for an NLRB election, file NLRB unfair labor practice charges and ask for an election at the same time. It may be several days or weeks before the picketing can be stopped.

16. If the union threatens anyone with violence, unfair labor practices should be charged, local police should be alerted, and a state court injunction against such violations should be sought.
17. Do not recognize the union on the basis of an informal poll. Ask for an NLRB election.
18. Prepare job descriptions for all managers and foremen and for all clerical, technical, and professional employees.
19. Do not carry on a campaign of home visits to dissuade employees from joining the union. Home visits by employers are considered to be coercive and illegal. Management's campaign should be limited to speeches, letters, circulars, and so on.
20. During the 24-hour period immediately preceding an NLRB election, do not make election speeches to the employees. Last-minute letters or circulars are permitted.
21. When arranging an NLRB election, care should be exercised to avoid confusing language in describing those employees eligible to vote as well as of those who are not eligible. The voting unit will become the bargaining unit if the union wins the election.
22. Understand that the law considers foremen representatives and agents of management and the management will therefore be held responsible if foremen threaten or coerce employees who are sympathetic to the union.
23. Understand that foremen's expressions of their own opinions that are not intimidating or coercive are permitted. They should in fact be encouraged.
24. Be wary of making changes in pay rates or working conditions.
25. In borderline cases, where employees may or may not be eligible to vote, weigh the advantage of having them vote against the disadvantage of having them permanently included in the unit if the union wins the election.
26. Avoid actions that might provide the union with a basis for unfair labor practice charges.
27. Keep in mind that unfair labor practice charges will delay an election unless they are waived for the purpose of

setting aside the vote. If there is a waiver, allow sufficient time before voting.

28. If employees are anxious about wage adjustments, explain that management's hands are tied during the organization effort.
29. Make it clear to employees that the law protects their right to join a union, but that it also protects them if they wish to stay out or vote against the union.
30. Stress the fact that NLRB balloting is secret. No one will ever know how an individual employee cast his vote.
31. Urge employees to vote. The result is determined on the basis of the majority of those voting, not a majority of those in the unit eligible to vote.
32. Wage a vigorous campaign, but do not build up a record of anti-union feeling. The company may have to negotiate a contract with the union as representatives of the employees.

As has been stated, the National Labor Relations Act of 1935 was the first statement of public policy regarding organized labor on a national scale. It stipulated that workers had the right to join a union if they were employed by a company whose activity affected interstate commerce, set up the machinery whereby the union could gain National Labor Relations Board certification as the representative group, and demanded that management and union bargain collectively for pay, hours, and working conditions. In addition, the Act classified five management actions as "unfair labor practices":

1. Interfering with the right of employees to form, join, or assist labor organizations and to bargain collectively.
2. Dominating or interfering with the formation or administration of a labor union or contributing financial support to the union.
3. Discriminating against employees who are active unionists.
4. Discharging or otherwise discriminating against an employee because he has filed charges or given testimony under the Act.
5. Refusing to bargain with employee representatives.

The National Labor Relations Board has enforced these provisions very rigidly by issuing "cease and desist" orders to managements found guilty of one or more of the practices cited. The law did not set forth any of the rights and privileges of management nor did it cover union actions which might be called unfair.

The effect of this Act, of course, was to place severe limitations on management, particularly the foreman. In fact, most foremen, to avoid difficulties for their companies and themselves, have adopted a "see nothing, hear nothing, say nothing" attitude, particularly during a union organizing effort. However, in 1947 the Act was amended by the passage of the so-called Taft-Hartley Act, which contains seven unfair practices on the part of unions.

Under Taft-Hartley, the union may not—

1. Coerce employees into union membership by such tactics as threats against employers, interference by mass picketing, or any other strong-arm methods.
2. Coerce employers in their choice of collective bargaining and grievance-handling representatives.
3. Force or attempt to force an employer to discriminate against employees for activity on behalf of a rival union or for failure to join a union.
4. Refuse to bargain collectively in good faith.
5. Engage in secondary strikes and boycotts.
6. Levy excessive or discriminatory initiation fees even though there is a valid union shop agreement.
7. Attempt to force an employer to pay for work not performed (featherbedding).

In conclusion, it may be said that since 1935 much has been learned about labor-management relations. There is a better balance between labor and management. There are still strikes and other labor difficulties, but the issues are not the same ones that they were 30 years ago. Both union officials and management personnel have matured to a better understanding of each other. This has given the foreman more freedom than he had in 1935 and the years immediately following. Even so, the foreman should know the rules of the game.

16

LIVING WITH THE
CONTRACT

In his own department, a union contract, even though it may be classified as "shop law," is largely what the foreman makes it. It is what the contract *does* that is important, not only what it *is;* and how the foreman applies it determines to a large degree what it does. The foreman who is a true management representative (as he should be) and who fully understands what the union contract means to management can use it to promote good relations with his employees and union officials, particularly the department's union steward.

This may seem like an easy assignment—and, in fact, it isn't too difficult when the contract states specifically what is to be done in a given situation. But a union contract is seldom that specific, largely because many situations that will arise on the shop floor cannot be foreseen at the time the contract is negotiated. Therefore, the foreman must use his own judgment; his decisions make the contract a success or a failure in his department.

Before the foreman can be held responsible for administration of a contract, he should be given an opportunity to participate in pre-negotiation meetings. If the company is negotiating its first contract, the foreman should be in a position to offer suggestions from his experience with other contracts. If a current contract is expiring, he should certainly be able to make recommendations for the next one which will ease or eliminate some of the problems which he has had to face under the present one.

As a matter of fact, however, the foreman is seldom invited to participate in prenegotiation meetings; and, if by some chance he is asked, he seldom can be of much help, not because he lacks intelligence, but primarily because he feels that he can do nothing much anyway. Probably he has kept no record of the problems that have arisen. The only thing he can do, if asked, is to make general suggestions depending on what he can remember. Foremen who are denied involvement and influence lack the skills needed for participation in prenegotiation work although individual foremen naturally differ in their abilities.

Whether the foreman is kept abreast of the progress of negotiations or not, once the contract has been negotiated and completed he should be thoroughly briefed on all its provisions: what they mean, and how management expects them to be interpreted. The foreman will do a better job of administering a contract when he knows the reason for a provision and the intent of both parties at the time of negotiation. This kind of briefing, however, still leaves the foreman in need of clarification on some of the contract points which he will have to deal with on his job. When necessary, the foreman should therefore feel free to seek advice and guidance from management.

Working with a union should make a good foreman a better foreman. American management in general has improved its handling of unions and union contracts, and out of this experience, certain "ground rules" have developed that the foreman should review and implement, particularly if operating under a union contract is a new experience for him.

The Union Steward

In the first place, it must be recognized that for every foreman there is a union steward or shop committeeman in the same department. A job for the foreman, obviously, is to develop a good working relationship with this steward. The union steward is elected to his position by the same men who are the foreman's employees, and the steward is very sensitive to the problems and complaints of his constituency.

The foreman's difficulties are almost directly proportional to the amount of control that the union steward has in the department. If the foreman is too easy, the union steward will take over. As management "backs off" or abdicates in the exercise of its right to manage a department, plant, or company, the union will move in to fill the gap. There can be no power vacuum. On the other hand, if the foreman is a harsh "whip cracker," the union steward will harass him with grievances and complaints. Between the two extremes is the area of effective management created by prompt attention to the bona fide problems brought up by the steward.

Here are suggestions which should help the foreman to arrive at a good working relationship with the department steward:

1. While the foreman should seek the advice of others in the management when he needs clarification of contract provisions, he should also be interested in the steward's views. Even though the steward may oppose him, he will appreciate being asked.
2. The foreman should be sure that all new employees meet the steward and understand his role.
3. Although most contracts do not require it, the foreman should tell the steward about disciplinary action before it is taken. This is simply a matter of courtesy. If the steward disagrees with the action, he may submit a grievance afterward.
4. Since nothing frustrates and antagonizes people more than prolonged delay, the foreman should respond courteously and promptly to the steward's complaints and grievances. This is particularly important when he has promised to reply at some future time.
5. Above all, the foreman should never speak disparagingly of or to the steward in the presence of other employees. Any act that damages the steward's image in the eyes of his own fellow workers can make for a very difficult working relationship.
6. A new foreman might well consider asking the steward's opinion about some of the men in order to prevent future

problems. A steward who has known the men for some time should have some good tips to offer.

Contract Provisions

There are other ground rules for operating under a union contract. For instance:

1. Most contracts provide for a period (a minimum of 30 days) after hire during which the union has no jurisdiction over a new employee. The foreman should explain the terms of this probationary period and see that the new employee's performance reaches a level that will allow him to become a "regular" employee at the expiration of the stated number of days.
2. If the employee is engaged for part-time, temporary, or seasonal work, the foreman should make certain that his status is clear to him when he is hired.
3. Company rules and policies should be understood by all employees. The foreman should administer these rules equitably, without discrimination or favoritism.
4. Each department foreman should cooperate with the foremen of other departments in the uniform administration of rules and contract provisions.
5. The foreman should observe the time limits stipulated in the contract and be sure that the union steward does the same.
6. All foremen should take advantage of any opportunity to learn more about the handling of grievances, the maintenance of adequate records, and the administration of discipline.
7. As much as he can, the foreman should review, revise, and update personnel practices in such areas as hiring and induction, rotation and interchange of employees, performance review, standards of performance, counseling, and training of employees.
8. The foreman should recognize that a grievance decision may be setting a precedent for the next case that arises.

9. The foreman should act to have outdated, invalid rules deleted. No worker should get the impression that any rule can be ignored; bad rules should simply not exist.
10. Expedient contract administration should be avoided except in an emergency. The expedient answer for the short run is usually not adequate for the long run.
11. A good foreman will get all the facts before making a decision. If the decision is fair and proper, he should stick to it, even through threats and shouting. Sometimes arbitration is necessary and welcome to resolve ambiguous language or to establish a *modus operandi.*

Grievance Machinery—Arbitration

The union has two basic jobs, which bring it into existence and keep it alive:

1. To bargain with the employer for wages, hours, and conditions of employment.
2. To protect and defend its members.

Inasmuch as the foreman probably has had no direct voice in the actual bargaining and must operate daily under the resulting contract, he must be constantly aware of the second objective of the union when he makes his decisions.

Most contracts outline the steps through which the employee and his union must proceed in carrying a grievance to its conclusion. First, the grievance is presented to the foreman for consideration and adjustment. (See Chapter 7.) In the hands of well-trained, management-minded foremen, 85 percent of all grievances should be settled at this level. However, in practice many grievances are not settled satisfactorily by the first-line foreman, and the contract provides that an unsatisfied grievance may then be brought before an impartial arbitrator, umpire, or panel of arbitrators. The decision made at this point is final and binding on both parties. It is therefore important that the foreman, when trying to settle differences, keep one eye on the ever-present possibility that the case may go to arbitration. Since he may have to be present during the arbitration session, he should know something about the format.

Labor arbitration is a quasi-judicial procedure, basically similar to an informal courtroom trial. Each side agrees to abide by the decision, and if either party refuses to do so, the other party may refer it to a court for correction. Both parties may be represented by attorneys, but the union does not bring in attorneys as frequently or as quickly as does management.

Most arbitration hearings start with a presentation by one party and a reply by the other. Each side then has witnesses, documentary evidence, and so on, to prove its case in direct examination. All evidence and witnesses are subject to cross-examination by the other party. The hearing is concluded by summaries by each side, with written briefs submitted on occasion. The arbitrator, after examining and considering the case, issues his decision (award).

Foremen do not enjoy appearing in arbitration, offering testimony, or especially being subjected to cross-examination by the union. The union tries to open up holes in the foreman's testimony and make him "lose his cool." When it succeeds, the foreman becomes his own worst enemy.

Of the many thousands of cases which management loses in arbitration, most are lost because of lack of documentary evidence. It is particularly important, therefore, that the foreman record and file all his actions. The union and the employee involved should also have copies of the statement. This is particularly important when the employee is warned of suspension or discharge in the event of another violation. Frequently, when the union receives its copy of this warning, it will investigate the case at that point. Many times when the foreman has been justified, and there is documentary proof in the files, the union will tell the employee to improve his conduct because the union will not defend him if he is fired. The employee usually does reform in such a situation.

An actual case, which almost went to arbitration, shows the need for documentary evidence. It involves an employee who knowingly violated a rule.

October 3, 1968. The foreman sent a letter to the employee telling him of his violation and repeating what the foreman had told him in the way of a mild reprimand. A copy was sent to the union.

January 17, 1969. The foreman sent a letter to the employee telling of his second violation of the same rule, with an additional statement that the company could not continue to let him violate it.

January 22, 1969. After another violation, the foreman sent a letter to the employee stating that because of the two prior warnings, he was discharged as of that day.

January 23, 1969. The discharged employee registered a grievance contesting the discharge. He had full union support.

This grievance could have gone to arbitration. The company was advised that its position was very weak; if the case were arbitrated, the arbitrator would probably reinstate the man with some or all of his back pay. The company's weakness lay in the fact that, while the discharging letter mentioned two prior warnings, the evidence proved that the employee had only be *reprimanded,* never *warned.* In a meeting with the union, the company acknowledged this point and converted the discharge into a short-time suspension without pay. The suspension included a warning that another violation of the same kind would bring immediate discharge of the employee.

Had the company lost this case (as there was every reason to believe that it would), the payment of back wages would have been a relatively small matter, even though the amount could have run to several thousands of dollars. The major concern would have been the serious damage to the foreman's influence and prestige. This foreman apparently did not know the difference between a reprimand and a warning. Actually, the new union steward was the employee involved, and he was testing the foreman to see how much power the new union had.

Seniority Clauses

There are other union situations in which the foreman must produce documented factual records. The contract seniority clause, which calls for posting an open job and allowing the most senior employee who bids to fill the job, can be a tremendous burden to the foreman. Here is an example of such a clause:

Strict seniority shall prevail in choice of vacation, layoff, rehiring, jobs with higher pay, better jobs of equal pay, and the right to bid on job classification as set forth in this Agreement. Seniority shall be determined on the length of service of the employee. The date of the last hiring of an employee shall determine his seniority, and the company payroll records of employment shall determine the date of employment and the order of seniority.

Seniority is based on the concept that an employee with years of service should not be threatened by a man of lesser service or a new hire, even though either of them may have greater skills. Seniority was originally intended to be, not an advantage, but only a protection against being placed at a disadvantage.

The preceding contract clause, which actually exists in a contract as of this writing, can cause chaos in a department. What are some of the problems that can arise?

Suppose that a top job in a department becomes open and the foreman posts the job on the bulletin board. (Incidentally, the clause does not specify how long the job must be posted.) Five men apply for it. Among them is John Jones; and, since he has the most service, the foreman must give him the job. Jones may or may not be qualified, and there is no time stipulated within which he must become qualified. However, the job which Jones left is now unfilled, and it too must be posted. Again a group bids; the senior man gets it; and his job, now also open, must be posted. And so on and on. A foreman cannot assign a man to an open job unless there are no bidders. Only after all posted jobs in the chain have been filled may the foreman hire a new man to fill the last and probably the lowest job. In some cases, when the union covers all employees down to and including the janitorial force, the seniority provision has no limits and the only jobs left open for hire are the janitors' jobs. All new workers are hired as janitors, and they move up from there. It is even conceivable that a wholly unskilled janitor who had great seniority could bid for and get a much higher job for which he was quite unqualified. Furthermore, since no time must elapse before a man may bid again, men can change jobs every few weeks.

Nevertheless, this is the sort of contract clause under which the foreman must operate his department. But he does not have to resign himself to chaos forever. Every union contract has a stipulated life, at which point it is open for negotiation and change. In the case, just related, of an open-end seniority provision with unlimited bidding, the foreman can and must do something to improve the situation.

His greatest aid in the removal of this or any other burdensome contract provision is to keep a complete written record of every move that is made—by date, name of employee, change of classification, time involved, amount of training involved, cost of reduced production and damaged product, and any other relevant items. For example, if in the life of a contract (say, two years) five open upper-grade jobs triggered a total of 47 job changes (several men changing several times, with all the attendant costs), management would be in a better position to bargain for improvement—especially if more than one foreman kept records.

The Foreman's Potential Role

So, even though the foreman may not sit at the bargaining table, he can make his voice heard and his needs known in collective bargaining negotiations if he knows what to do and will take the time to do it. Furthermore, the more factual information management has for the next negotiations, the better it can present a counterproposal to the union's demands and the better its position will be.

To test his understanding and knowledge of his union contract, a foreman might ask himself these questions:

1. If a man is changed to a job paying a higher or lower rate, when does his rate change?
2. Can the foreman increase or reduce his workforce freely?
3. Does the union contract force a reduction in the workweek or allow for layoffs?
4. Under what conditions may a foreman do the work of those in the bargaining unit?
5. Is the foreman allowed to introduce new and improved methods of work?
6. Can the union prohibit the installation of new methods?
7. Must all laid-off personnel be recalled before new people are hired?
8. Can the foreman always promote the best-qualified man?

9. Must the senior man bidding for a posted job be given a trial period? If so, how long is it?
10. Under the union contract, can the foreman adjust crew sizes?
11. Must employees work overtime when required?
12. Is there a penalty if they don't work overtime?
13. Is overtime provided on a rotational basis, so as to provide opportunity for all to earn extra income, or because actual work must be done?
14. What questions are prohibited from going to arbitration?
15. Can the foreman hire his own men?
16. Is the union compelled to admit all new people to membership?
17. Does the union contract distinguish between grievances that may go to arbitration and those that may not?
18. In a series of jobs opened up through posting and bidding, how long must the foreman wait before assigning a man to a particular job?
19. What is the qualifying date for vacations?
20. What are the qualifications for a paid holiday?
21. How is seniority defined, and how may an employee lose seniority?
22. Is there a time limit within which a foreman must respond to a grievance?
23. If an employee is transferred to a job within the company but outside the bargaining unit, what happens to his seniority if he returns to his original job within the bargain-unit?
24. Does the 30-day probationary period in the union contract refer to working days or calendar days?

There are undoubtedly many other questions which the foreman could ask himself, but these are a start. If the foreman is in doubt about any of the answers, he should seek help. Even those of his answers which he believes to be correct should be checked by higher authority.

Of all of the duties and responsibilities of the true managerial foreman in a small company, one of the most important is that of administering the union contract as a manager. In the very large mass-production industries, such as automobile or steel, the foreman on the assembly line has little or nothing to do with the union contract under which he is living. It is doubtful that an employee will ever come to him with a grievance. He does little in the way of training new employees and has virtually nothing to say about hiring them. He is concerned solely with having the correct number of men "on the line," each of whom can do his portion of the total job adequately and rapidly enough to keep the product going by at a certain rate per minute. He is really not a foreman in the full sense of the term; in fact, he is much more of a monitor than a manager.

This condition did not always prevail. It has been brought about in large measure by the tremendous growth of these industries and the industrial unions within them. But another contributing element has been the foreman himself: He permitted it to happen. He did not develop rapidly enough to meet the rapidly changing conditions, and, meanwhile, the companies added staff people in all areas of management who mostly seem to be doing much of what the foreman should do.

This is not the case in smaller plants and industries at the present time, although it may well come about if the foreman either abdicates what management functions he now has or if he fails to develop to the point where he can handle additional responsibilites as the need arises. Certainly the foreman must now be able to administer a union contract if he is to be not only a good manager within his department but also a candidate for promotion to higher levels of management.

17

COST REDUCTION AND CONTROL

Every person in management today, whether he is a foreman or chairman of the board, recognizes that more and more attention is necessarily being devoted to the costs of producing and distributing goods and services. American industry has undergone drastic changes since the early 1940's, when it was called upon to perform miracles, regardless of cost, during World War II. At that time, the government was the primary consumer in an emergency so great that cost was no factor. All that mattered was the ability to produce in as short a time as possible. And it is true that American business did an outstanding job.

However, since World War II, business in general has been faced with outside economic forces. For example:

1. A constant and seemingly irreversible rise in the cost of the materials and services which management must buy to manufacture its products.
2. Increasing customer resistance to constantly rising prices.
3. Greatly increased competition due to (1) the enlarged population and its demands for goods and services and (2) the

development of thousands of new products and services which were not available a decade ago.

At the same time, American management has been under other pressures, mostly internal, such as these:

1. Stockholders want a reasonable return on their investment and become impatient if the return is unsteady or intermittent.
2. Employees want and obtain constantly increasing wages and fringe benefits.
3. Consumers want reasonable prices within their economic reach.

It seems that the events of the past quarter-century have caused American business to shift from a philosophy of providing products and services, without regard to cost, to one of making products and services available at the lowest possible cost. It follows that continuing activity and alertness in controlling and reducing costs are no longer a matter of choice (if they ever were) but are strictly a *must* for survival.

A glance at recent surveys of reasons for business failures reveals that most fall under the heading of "poor management." While this is a broad term, it can usually be applied when management has become so complacent and self-satisfied that it feels rising costs can easily be passed on to the consumer; when management doesn't know what the conditions are or, even if it did know, wouldn't know what to do about them.

Virtually all companies are in highly competitive markets and pay about the same price for the basic elements of men, money, machinery, and materials. If these four important elements have the same cost in any competitive industry or business, the only way a firm can compete and remain alive at a reasonable profit is to use these principal resources more effectively. This does not mean that a special "program" or "campaign" should be mounted by a general manager, plant manager, or foreman along his regular duties. It does mean that cost control and good management go hand in hand. The one is a by-product of the other; it cannot exist alone.

It becomes increasingly apparent that foremen should have some understanding of how production costs are computed and which items go into the cost of production. This is not to say that the foreman is expected to become an expert cost accountant, but he should have a sufficient appreciation of cost accounting to analyze statements pertaining to his department and thereby increase his ability to get out production at the lowest cost consistent with good quality and quantity.

Cost Categories

In manufacturing, the costs in a particular producing department are generally divided into two major categories—prime manufacturing costs and overhead. Prime manufacturing costs are made up of direct materials and direct labor, while overhead consists of manufacturing or departmental burden and administrative or general expense.

Direct material is only that which goes into the manufacture of the finished product. For example, if a company manufactures wooden toys, the wood used in erecting wall partitions does not enter into the manufacture of the product and therefore is not charged as direct material. Direct labor is the total payroll of all those employees engaged in actually making the product; this does not include foremen, maintenance men, or janitors.

Manufacturing or department burden (sometimes called shop expense) includes all factory or department expense other than direct materials and direct labor and administrative or general expense. A typical example is the cost of heat, light, power, and other utilities which a manufacturing department requires and for which it must pay. Indirect labor, such as the foreman's salary, also is part of department burden, as is the department's share of rent for the space it occupies. If the department has its own office with a clerk, this too belongs in department burden.

Administrative or general expense (overhead) includes management salaries, general office expense, and other items which cannot be directly charged to the shop, but for which each department must pay its share. Each company has its own formula for spreading overhead over the manufacturing departments. Usually, it is made up of items over which the plant or department foremen have little direct control.

Cost Accounting

Systematic cost accounting is a device for measuring the effectiveness of the whole company or a particular department; it eliminates guesswork. For general management, cost accounting is useful in—

1. Establishing the selling price of a product to insure a safe profit.
2. Determining which products are the best profit producers.
3. Preparing tax-return statements.

For the department foreman, cost accounting assists in—

1. Determining reasonable standards of work and pay.
2. Providing comparative costs of various products or orders as checks on efficiency.
3. Furnishing the foreman with cost reports which are helpful guides in controlling costs.

If cost reports are to be valuable to the foreman or anyone else, they must be reliable representations of the facts. From this it follows that records must be accurate and well kept. This involves the foreman.

For adequate control, the foreman cannot limit himself to a review of a cost report which he has received and still satisfy himself that an item included on it is "good," "fair," or otherwise unless he has something with which to compare it. Such terms as "good" are relative; good as compared with what? Therefore, he should set up goals or standards for each item of variable cost for which he is responsible. He can arrive at these goals by himself or, better, in conjunction with his lead people or even all his employees.

For example, in most manufacturing enterprises each producing department turns out its part or finished product, but everything coming off the end of the line will not be usable or salable. What is not is known by various shop terms: scrap, shrinkage, cripples, manufacturing rejects, and the like. Part may be salvaged, part may be sold at reduced prices, and part will have to be discarded. In any case, it cannot be classified as perfect, and the more of it there is, the greater the cost of good product will be if all other costs remain the same. A goal should therefore be established showing in dollars, units, or a percentage the acceptable amount of poor product per hour, day, or week. By comparing the actual figure against this goal, the foreman will know immediately whether he is "in line" and the item is under control. If a similar goal is set for each cost factor, the foreman and the entire department will know how well they are doing.

Three-Step Program

Some foremen do an excellent job of telling their people why costs must be cut and getting up a full head of steam to tackle the job of reducing waste. Yet, in many cases, they get nowhere because they have failed to determine—

1. Where the waste is occurring.
2. Why the waste is occurring.
3. How it can be prevented.

Costs can never be reduced unless the foreman applies considerable analytical thinking to these three problems.

To assist in controlling and reducing costs, the following three steps are suggested:

1. *Find the target.* To hit a target, the foreman and his employees have to know where it is located. What are the scrap losses? How much and what kind of materials are involved? Which materials are being used in excess of a predetermined standard amount?
2. *Pinpoint the cause.* Now the foreman must find the specific cause or causes for the waste. Is it employee carelessness?

Poor supervision? Inadequate instruction? Defective material? Faulty design? Improper use of machinery? The real trouble must be "bird-dogged" out.

3. *Determine the remedy.* After the waste has been located and the cause determined, the foreman is in a position to prevent it from recurring. In most cases, the cause will suggest the remedy.

The specific means of preventing recurrence will vary with individual circumstances. However, there are a few general measures that have proved effective in reducing losses of almost any kind.

Set goals. This is of paramount importance. What is the present loss from scrap or other waste? What is the target the foreman would like to hit? Make meeting it a challenge and not a threat.

Encourage participation. The foreman should enlist the support and participation of all the employees. Get their suggestions for improvement. Get them on the team and keep them there by convincing them that any reduction of excessive costs is in their own interests.

Dramatize. Put the actual materials and supplies on display with price tags on them. Show the spoiled part or product labeled with the actual cost. Indicate how many good products have to be made and sold to pay for one bad product.

Praise, encourage, discipline. Employees who do a good job of reducing cost deserve praise and should receive it. Others may have to be encouraged to do better. Still others, unfortunately, may have to be disciplined if they deliberately waste materials or supplies, and will not cooperate. However, most employees want to do a better job, given the opportunity.

Maintain interest. Keep the employees informed of their progress. When goals are reached, don't call the battle off. Now the objective is to stay at this level. Analysis must continue to determine the cause of failure and to make corrections.

Areas for Attention. There are many areas for better cost control and cost reduction which should get the attention of the foreman. Exhibit 18 is a list of suggested possible causes of waste and what the foreman can do about them.

Exhibit 18

Waste and Its Remedies

MATERIALS

Possible Cause	*What to Do*
Too much on hand.	Requisition as needed.
Loose checking of amounts received, on hand, or produced.	Tighten up system to prevent loss and theft.
Careless storage.	Pile and store properly.
	Protect material from injury.
	Assign and train responsible storeroom clerk.
Unnecessary scrapping.	Salvage everything of value.
	Find other uses for obsolete material.
Backtracking—not a continuous flow.	Rearrange routing.
Excessive spoilage in processing.	Set goals to allow as little as possible.

EQUIPMENT AND MACHINERY

Rust, dirt, dust, fumes.	Inspect regularly.
	Provide adequate protection.
	Clean periodically.
Breakdowns.	Provide preventive maintenance and lubrication.
	Avoid "temporary" repairs.
Improper use, overloading.	Use for purpose intended.
	Do not overload.
	Instruct employees not to abuse.
Too much equipment.	Keep to a minimum.
	Use to capacity or eliminate.
Unnecessary scrapping.	Repair if worthwhile.

TOOLS AND SUPPLIES

Personal usage.	Provide inventory control.
	Discipline violators.

Exhibit 18 (*continued*)

Extravagant use (too much or wrong purpose).	Encourage thrift. Tighten control. Order supplies designed for specific purposes.
Poor storage or holding devices.	Provide containers or equipment. Control outgo.

POWER, HEAT, AND LIGHT

Machinery running, heat and light on when not needed.	Train workers to conserve. Provide closer inspection.
Leaky valves, pipes, or fittings.	Investigate regularly and repair or change.
Improper conveyor system.	Use gravity wherever possible.

SPACE

Storage of material which should be scrapped.	Remove or dispose of.
Unnecessary materials at workplace.	Reduce or improve stock deliveries.
Unused equipment taking up valuable space.	Store or junk.
Ladders, trucks, or other materials in the way of other workers.	Keep passageways clear. Train workers to cooperate.
Insufficient lighting.	Eliminate dark spots.

TIME AND EFFORT

Excessive handling or conveying. Use of men instead of machines.	Reroute or reduce steps. Use power and machinery. Eliminate heavy lifting and carrying. Use platforms in unloading.
Workers waiting for materials.	Improve deliveries.
Wrong placement of equipment.	Rearrange for greater convenience.
Poor scheduling of operators.	Plan more precisely.
Inadequate elevator service.	Provide improvement.

In addition to these and similar *specific* causes of loss or waste, there are other *general* causes to be found in many shops, offices, and nonproducing departments. Out of the hundreds that exist, only a relatively few can be listed:

1. Employees do not know the money cost of machinery, tools, materials, scrap, or utilities.
2. The employees have been poorly instructed in use and care of equipment.
3. The foreman has not set a good example.
4. There is no system to control pilferage.
5. There is a lack of cooperation with the maintenance department.
6. Long-distance telephone calls are made when a letter would serve.
7. Off-again, on-again campaigns of cost reduction are conducted without consistent stress on the necessity to keep costs at a minimum.
8. Wasteful practices are permitted in order to meet production schedules.
9. Inventory control is loose.
10. Supplies are open to any employee; they are not "on issue."
11. The foreman fails to seek the advice and assistance of other management people in determining the corrective action to take.
12. Housekeeping is poor.
13. Hoarding of supplies results in obsolescence.
14. Machine failures are not reported promptly.
15. The foreman does not know the skills, interests, and physical capacity of his individual employees.
16. Labor turnover is excessive.
17. Employees are not familiar with quality and quantity standards.
18. Working conditions are poor.
19. Wasteful and useless motions have not been eliminated through job study.
20. Selection of new employees is haphazard.
21. Grievances have not been handled promptly, causing unrest and reduced work effort.
22. The foreman has not followed through after correcting

practices that result in excessive costs, thus allowing inefficiencies to creep back into the department.
23. Excessive absence and tardiness of employees is a problem. This is of such great importance to labor costs that the balance of this chapter will be devoted to it.

Payroll Expense

Because, in a great many industries, the payroll is the biggest dollar item in production costs, the factors of employee selection, orientation, training, and motivation become important in any cost control effort. Inept or misplaced people who make expensive errors, waste time, and complicate the work of others can cost thousands of dollars in a year.

Nonetheless, an effective program of selection, training, and motivation is not enough to insure maximum control of payroll expense. Much is being done—and should be—in these important areas to impress upon the employee the fact that he is obligated to be present regularly and punctually. Yet some workers are frequently absent, and others are often late.

Many production employees who receive no pay for the time they do not work are inclined to feel that, because they are not paid, their absence or tardiness costs the company nothing. Unless the situation is pointed out, they do not realize that their lack of dependability requires the company to maintain an excessively large workforce simply to get the job done. Moreover, they fail to see that the time lost by other employees, the slowness occasioned by reassignment to less familar work, and the increase in spoilage all cost money and, eventually, loss of their own efficiency.

Tardiness. Besides the time-honored reasons for tardiness (such as alarm clock failures or sleeping through the alarm), there are the more modern excuses of traffic congestion and other transportation difficulties. Sickness at home, too much overtime, poor health, and change of hours are of course hardy perennials. A careful analysis of each situation will tell the foreman whether the cause may not actually be laziness, indifference, exhaustion from a "moonlight" job, worry, or the foreman's bad example.

While it is true that the tardy employee loses a certain amount of pay for the late time, it should be pointed out to him that he will experience further losses if his tardiness continues and he arrives later and later. Not only will he in all probability lose interest in his job, but the company will certainly lose its interest in him as a prospect for advancement; at best, he will be rated as indifferent, unreliable, and a poor example to others. In any case, tardiness—except in an emergency—cannot be condoned. Steps must be taken to reduce it and the excessive costs which go with it. If all fails, the chronically tardy employee must be fired.

Of the many things which the foreman can do to reduce tardiness, the first is that he be punctual himself. To repeat: There is no substitute for a good example by the leader. What else can he do? If there are transportation difficulties, the foreman may recommend the provision of adequate facilities by the company or the establishment of car pools by the employees. He may help to relocate employees nearer to the plant or, when poor planning is the real culprit, simply advise leaving home earlier. Many employees who live in the suburbs and use public transportation have found that the facilities are not as reliable as they were some time ago. These people must leave home earlier in order to to arrive at work on time.

Bad storms or slippery roads may hold up some of the workforce. However, some employees (using the same roads) inevitably are on time while others are not. In most instances, those who arrive punctually start earlier, allowing time for contingencies.

Sometimes a warning of disciplinary action may jolt an employee into a greater degree of alertness and reduce his tardiness. This of course is appropriate only to tardiness which is due to indifference, lack of ambition, habit, or excessive moonlighting. But a tactful foreman may, through his personal interest, uncover and overcome many cases of lateness caused by worry over family and other problems.

When combined with the personal attention of the foreman, but not as a substitute for it, various plans to reduce tardiness have operated with different degrees of success. Some plants pay a cash bonus to employees who are consistently punctual for a certain period of time. The amount usually depends on wages during the same period. This may be called a positive method of reducing tardiness, but it has its weaknesses. In the first place, the employee may be late owing to an emergency beyond his control early in the bonus period, so that he receives no portion of the punctuality bonus for the balance of the period. In the second place—and this is a more serious defect—the plan violates the principle of payment for value received since it pays employees additional money for doing something which they should be doing anyway as an implicit part of their employment obligations—attending regularly and on time.

Some companies have reduced lateness by posting departmental punctuality averages. Competition between departments and departmental pride are played up. This is a constructive plan for offsetting and correcting tardiness, but it, too, has a negative side. Since it focuses departmental attention on the tardy employee, he may incur the disfavor of the other workers in the department.

A simple monthly chart of tardiness and absence should be made and kept in sight in the foreman's office (see Exhibit 19). The very existence of any such control chart will in itself improve the record as soon as the employees know of it and realize that the foreman is watching it.

No plan devised to correct tardiness can do very much unless the foreman gives it his personal supervision. The best way to reduce tardiness is for the foreman to have a friendly, constructive talk with each offender, point out how his behavior affects others, and see that he realizes his responsibility to the company and to himself and help him to appreciate the benefits to be gained from consistent punctuality.

Absenteeism. "Absenteeism" is a broad term which covers the failure of employees, for whatever reason, to report for work as scheduled. There are two kinds of absenteeism: (1) involuntary absences, over which the worker has no control, and (2) voluntary absenteeism, when the worker could be at work if he chose to be but has chosen not to be. The foreman may not be able to do much to control involuntary absences, but he can do a great deal to reduce voluntary absenteeism.

Absence represents the same loss that tardiness does to the absent employee, to other employees in the department, and to the company. In addition to his lost wages, the habitual absentee loses his personal integrity and morale. He finds himself rated below steady employees who have the same abilities and thus loses his eligibility for advancement. He may miss out on merit increases and be put at the head of the list for layoff or dismissal. When sickness or some other unfortunate circumstance keeps a steady employee away from work, his good attendance record supports him; but the

Exhibit 19

Absence and Tardiness Chart

Month _____ 19___

Department _____

NAME	1	2	3	4	5	6	7	8	9	10	11	12	13	14	15	16	17	18	19	20	21	22	23	24	25	26	27	28	29	30	31	MINUTES LATE

O   Late
NX Unexcused absence
V   Vacation

OC Excused absence
LV Leave of absence
LD Layoff, disciplinary

LP Layoff, production
U   Unreported absence
C   Compensation case

1 1st shift
2 2nd shift
3 3rd shift

chronic absentee is not so fortunate since his absence, even when involuntary, simply adds to an already bad "track record."

Absenteeism can be controlled and reduced by the same methods used in combating tardiness. A practical measure is, again, the chart shown as Exhibit 19.

In some companies, the name of each absentee is sent by the foreman to the personnel office or to the superintendent or plant manager within the first hour after starting time. When required, the name may be sent to the company nurse or medical department in order that more information may be obtained about the absence before the man returns to work.

No absence should be taken lightly. All absentees should be interviewed by the foreman when they return to work. He should learn, if possible, the real reason for the absence. After excuses are discounted, necessary absences are usually found to be rare.

In talking with the employee, the foreman should point out that frequent absence handicaps the work of other employees and can injure one's own prospects for advancement. The employee should be encouraged to understand the value of his job and his place on the team. His pride in holding up his end of the work should be appealed to.

The company, plant, or department rules should specify (1) notifying the foreman in advance when an employee expects that he will have to be absent or (2) telephoning as soon as possible if an emergency arises. When a worker deliberately absents himself from the job without notifying his foreman, the latter must consider some disciplinary action. To ignore a case of this kind will surely lead to a complete breakdown of departmental discipline.

Rules and penalties are required for the small group of employees who do not respond to persuasion. The foreman should make certain that his employees know that the rules regarding absenteeism will be enforced firmly and fairly. If formal reprimands and other disciplinary measures fail to cure the chronic absentee, the foreman must start to think of discharge.

18

TYPICAL PERSONNEL PROBLEMS

This last chapter presents cases in which industrial foremen have encountered problems involving people. Some of the situations depicted have actually happened; others have been created for the purpose of provoking thought.

The statement of each case is followed by what might be considered an "answer." Actually there is no real answer because there is no "right" or "wrong" as there would be if foremanship were an exact science. The statements following each case are merely *opinions* of the author, even though many of them have been substantiated by other foremen. In all cases, the opinion was developed after the fact. This is known as "Monday morning quarterbacking." It is easy because the decision-making atmosphere is cool, quiet, and unencumbered by emotion.

If the foreman on the job can generate a similar atmosphere in which to think out the steps to be taken and allow his intelligence, rather than his emotions, to dictate his action, many situations will be resolved before they become ugly and difficult problems. The point to be remembered is that rational thought is almost impossible in an emotionally charged atmosphere; thus the problem solution arrived at is usually not a good one.

Case 1

Joe is the foreman of a crew of laborers. About a month ago, one of his new men, who at that time had only 12 weeks' service, complained of a sore back. Joe sent the man to the doctor for an examination. The doctor could find no sign of injury or history of illness, but thought it would be desirable to keep the man on light work "for a short time." Joe gave the man some light work which was not really necessary, but which served to keep the man on the payroll.

During the next month, the man maintained that his back was not improving and, on several occasions, objected to the suggestion that he resume his regular job. Joe overheard the man say to another, "The way to get a soft job is to pretend your back is hurt—they can't prove a thing!" Joe was then convinced that the man was a malingerer.

One day, a couple of transfers left Joe shorthanded, so he instructed the man to resume his old job. The man protested, refused to obey the order, and, when Joe insisted, became abusive. He swore at Joe and threatened to "report" him. Joe sent the man home, telling him that he was to be discharged and instructing him to get his pay the following day.

Before leaving the plant, the man stopped to talk things over with the superintendent, and the superintendent told him to report for a physical examination on the following day. The man inferred from this that the foreman's notice of discharge might be reversed. When he arrived the next day, he punched the time clock as usual and reported for work. He told Joe the superintendent had suggested that he could not be discharged. Joe put the man on light work, arranged to send him to the doctor for an examination later in the day, and voided the discharge order.

"For a short time" is a relative term and, by itself, means little. The doctor should have stated exactly how long the man was to remain on light work and when he should report for re-examination. Joe should have accepted the doctor's report until the second medical examination substantiated his opinion that the employee was a malingerer.

Joe certainly should have sent the man to the doctor for another examination before returning him to his regular job in the department. In the absence of medical approval, the man was justified in refusing to do heavy work. The fact that he was in his probationary period does not negate his position as an employee. No employee should be discharged because he complains of illness. And, while it was acceptable for the superintendent to talk with the employee, he should have consulted the foreman before advising the man to have a medical examination.

An employee who claims to be ill or injured should not be discharged without the approval of the superintendent, the industrial relations department, or the plant medical officer.

Case 2

Gus has been the foreman of a department for 17 years and is known throughout the company for his strictness. He is tough on his men but gets things done. Under pressure, he raises his voice, becomes increasingly profane, and criticizes his men excessively. Whenever an employee fails to follow Gus's directions closely, he is given either a terrific "bawling out" or, if possible, time off as a penalty.

Recently the department was expanded, and Gus made one of his men, Herb, an assistant foreman. Herb was a quiet, unassuming man of 40 who had been in the department for 12 years. He had the confidence and respect of the men and was a natural choice for the job.

A few weeks after this new appointment, Gus wanted to make a change in equipment which would result in more volume. This change, however, would mean more crowded and hazardous working conditions. Herb quietly informed Gus that he thought it was a bad move and stated his reasons, one of which was that the men would resent it. Gus immediately assumed that Herb's promotion had gone to his head. He walked about the shop, condemning Herb in a loud voice, vowing that he was still the boss, and swearing that he was going to run the department as he saw fit.

A majority of the employees came to Herb and told him that he was right and they were back of him. Gus became furious at this behavior and told Herb, "You can either do things my way or else get out."

Herb, as an assistant foreman, was right in discussing the hazards of the proposed move with his foreman. After a good, thorough discussion, Gus could have abandoned the idea until a more appropriate time, or he could have asked Herb how the change might be made with a minimum of difficulty and let Herb execute it.

In no case should a foreman undermine his assistant in the minds of the department's employees. Both Gus and his assistant lose in this kind of atmosphere, but Gus loses most.

Case 3

Bill has been employed by the company for 20 years and is regarded as one of the best men in his department. Bill has a younger brother, Tom, who has a bad reputation in the community because of a series of irresponsible acts and is generally regarded as being unreliable and dishonest.

One day Bill approached his foreman with a request that Tom be given a job in the department. He stated that, with proper guidance and steady work, Tom would prove to be a good employee since he was strong, energetic, and experienced. Furthermore, since this was the first big favor he has asked in 20 years, Bill believed that special consideration was due him.

The foreman did not want to hire Tom even though there were suitable jobs open and men were being employed. However, in order to avoid offending Bill, he stated that all hiring had to be done by the personnel office and that Bill should take Tom in to see the director of personnel. The foreman promised to call the director to "see what he could do" for Tom. Bill regarded this statement as a promise that Tom would be employed and made his plans accordingly. But the foreman spoke to the director of personnel "off the record" and suggested that Tom would not be a satisfactory employee.

When the personnel director rejected his brother's application, Bill felt that he had not been treated fairly. He had lost status in the eyes of his family and his friends. He became very resentful toward management and made an effort to influence other employees by his critical comments about the company.

This is an excellent example of an attempt to pass the buck. No foreman should give the impression that anyone else does the final hiring for his department.

The foreman could easily have offered to interview Bill's brother to make a preliminary determination of his qualifications and then referred him to the personnel office for a more exhaustive interview and check. In telling Bill that he would do this, the foreman should have made it clear that the offer to consider Tom seriously should not be construed as an offer of employment.

The off-the-record call to the personnel office was a mistake on the part of the foreman. If he felt strongly that Tom would not make a good employee, and could justify his feeling with up-to-date information, he should have told Bill so in the most tactful way possible.

No foreman, or any one else, can have his cake and eat it too.

Case 4

Bill is a foreman in a machine shop. For ten years, his crew has been known among the employees as a good one to work with. Bill has earned the goodwill and respect of his men through considerate and helpful supervision. His men have greater freedom and more privileges than other men in the plant, but they rarely abuse these. One of the privileges is that the men can "knock off" and go to the canteen for a cup of coffee whenever they wish. This practice has not interfered with the efficiency of the shop, and Bill's men have been meeting the production schedule easily.

Because of changes in the shop, however, Bill loses most of his old men and gets a number of employees from other departments. During the next few months, his discipinary problems increase tremendously. One man has to be discharged for insubordination, while others repeatedly are found loafing, making careless mistakes, and indulging in horseplay. Production in Bill's shop drops behind schedule even though the new men are highly skilled and able to do the work. Soon Bill finds it necessary to report some of the men for violations of plant rules.

After a month or so, Bill's superintendent tells him that he should cut down on the number of violation reports because his department looks bad in comparison with other departments. He also tells Bill that he should keep his men out of the canteen during working hours because some of them are reported to have walked through other departments flaunting their special status. Later, the older men come to Bill in a group and protest the loss of their so-called "rights," stating that their work is just as good as it ever was. Then some of the new men go "over Bill's head" to the superintendent with the charge that Bill is reporting new men for leaving their jobs to go to the canteen while he does not report the older men for doing the same thing.

Bill should not have allowed his original crew a special privilege (frequent visits to the canteen) that was not extended to all employees in the plant. Nevertheless he did, and the price he is having to pay for this error in judgment did not show up until the composition of the crew changed and rule violations on the part of the newer men came to light.

These newer men were testing Bill for the limits of his tolerance, as people so frequently do. Bill should have stopped the practice of frequent canteen visits at once and immediately started to report any violation of plant rules, including the canteen visits. An explanation of the reason for this change to the older men or to the entire crew could have eased the situation considerably. The older men probably would have policed the newer men in the hope that the withdrawn privilege would be reinstated.

The superintendent was wrong in telling Bill to reduce the number of violation reports because his department looked bad. The only way to reduce the number of reports would be to reduce the number of violations. Moreover, violation reports for their own sake can go on indefinitely and do no good. An employee should be counseled about any rule violation and corrective steps agreed upon between him and the foreman. If improvement is not forthcoming after one or more additional violations, the employee should be warned of the penalty for the next violation. The files should carry reports of all these measures.

Case 5

Bill is a loader in the warehouse of a shipping department. His duties consist of loading coils and sheets into cars. He has had two years of high school and some experience as a salesman, and he has been studying electricity at night school. He wants to be transferred to a job as helper in the electric shop so that he can advance in the electrical trade.

Bill's foreman has had difficulty in getting good men on his crew, so he is not pleased at the prospect of losing one of his best men. When Bill first requested a transfer, the foreman did not bother to have him fill out the regular request-for-transfer form; he just called the personnel office and the maintenance department to see if there were openings available. There were none at the time. Later, on two occasions, Bill repeated his request, and the foreman replied that there were no openings yet. The foreman, however, did not call the personnel office on either occasion to verify this statement.

A few days later another man on the crew was transferred to the electric shop. This man was not as well qualified for electrical work as Bill. He had gotten the transfer by applying at the personnel office and by going personally to see the foreman of the electric shop. Bill felt that he had been held back by his foreman and promptly began "pulling strings" in the electric shop and the personnel office to get the job he wanted. After a short time, he succeeded.

The foreman was criticized by his superintendent for "letting good men get out of the department." It was suggested that by giving promotions or raises it should be possible to keep them on the crew. The foreman called the director of personnel and the electric shop foreman to complain that he was being "raided." The director of personnel promised not to authorize any more transfers from this foreman's crew to other departments.

Here is an extremely shortsighted foreman. It is good policy to transfer men to the type of work which they are ambitious to do and for which they are acquiring training. The foreman must help his people to grow even though it may mean losing an occasional man from his department.

In this case, the foreman committed a serious error when he failed to have Bill go through the prescribed procedure in applying for a transfer. The difficulty was compounded later by the foreman's prevarications in response to Bill's repeated requests.

An employee should apply for a transfer only through his own foreman, not directly to the personnel office. The transfer should be made only after the employee's foreman, the personnel office, and the foreman of the other department have approved the move. A man who short-cuts this procedure should be told the correct method, but not necessarily reprimanded.

The superintendent should not have criticized the foreman for "losing" two men. It is unwise to give undeserved raises and promotions in the hope of preventing men from transferring to other departments. Such a hope is founded in the false belief that men work only for money.

Case 6

In Department X, the position of inspector has been filled by promotion from within for many years. It pays well and is regarded as an excellent job. Many men look forward to attaining it. Recently, however, this job has become more difficult and important because customer requirements are higher. Also, new processes require the inspector to have greater metallurgical knowledge, and new technical duties have been added to the job. In short, the position has gradually been changing until, now, only a trained metallurgist can handle it successfully.

For the past year, the regular inspectors have held their jobs only because they received special assistance from metallurgists who were not regularly assigned to the work. It has been rumored that all future vacancies will be filled by graduate metallurgists, but the foreman has continued to hold out to rank-and-file employees the hope of advancement to an inspector's job. Last week a vacancy occurred; and, to the men's surprise, an "outsider" came in from the metallurgical department to fill it.

The men are now resentful because the foreman allowed them to anticipate being promoted to a job which they can never hold. They feel that the company is denying them a deserved chance for advancement. They are uncooperative with the new inspector because he broke into their own line of promotion. The foreman is angry because management kept him in the dark about its intentions regarding the inspector's job. Morale is very low, and production is dropping.

The change in the qualifications required for the inspector's job surely did not happen overnight. This is borne out by the fact that for the past year the regular inspectors received special assistance from the trained metallurgists.

The foreman should have looked into the impending change, or he should have at least been aware that one was possible. By anticipating the change and determining the reasons for it, the foreman could have explained it to his men well in advance. Some of the men who aspired to be inspectors might have done some extra studying and become qualified. In any case, the change would have been less of a shock, and less resentment would have followed. The foreman need not have been kept in the dark if he had had the interests of his men at heart.

Rarely is inspection fully effective when the inspector is accountable to the foreman whose department is turning out the product being inspected. It could be that the company recognized this and used the need for greater technical qualifications as the excuse for changing the situation.

Case 7

Joe is the new foreman of a machine-shop group. Before being transferred to this job, he was an assistant foreman in another department. A few days after being transferred, Joe concluded that the role in his new situation of foreman was very different from what it had been in his former department.

In the old department, the foreman was very strict and saw to it that the men "knew their place"; in the new shop, the foreman and his men were more friendly and sociable. In the old department, the foreman never spoke to the men except to give orders or to ask questions; in the new shop, the foreman was expected to join the men in their usual conversation and joking. In the old department, the foreman never allowed a man in his office except on business; in the new shop, the foreman's office was used freely by the men as a clubhouse or lounge.

It was clear that in the new shop the relationship between the foreman and his men was entirely different. Joe examined the records. He found that productivity, grievances, accidents, and other similarly important factors in both shops were about equal. The different methods of foremanship apparently made no difference in performance.

Since Joe was accustomed to a policy of keeping his men from being too familiar with him, he decided to follow that policy in the new shop. In order to make the change easier, he assembled the men for a conference and explained his preference to them. The men were visibly disturbed at what appeared to be an unnecessary move on Joe's part.

Joe's new policy interfered with the habits of the men. For example, some of them were in the habit of eating their lunch in the foreman's office. When Joe told them to stay out so that he could work undisturbed, they were irritated. Although Joe was fair and just, men became increasingly resentful of his attitude. The morale of the entire crew grew worse. Productivity went down, and Joe did not know what to do about it.

It would have been foolish for Joe to try to duplicate the attitude and behavior of the foreman he replaced. No two men are alike, nor do they work quite alike.

This is a typical case of a new man coming into a group; the fact that the new man was the foreman makes little difference. He has to adjust to the men; the men have to adjust to him; and the group, including the foreman, will never be the same. This is not to say that it may not be a better mixture.

Adjustment takes time and requires planning, thought, and patience. It would have been much better for Joe to make no changes for a short period and then to make them one at a time.

Anyone in this position must realize that, since he is the new man in the group, the greatest change may have come in him— with a much lesser change in each of the others. Apparently, Joe expected that all the changing was to be done by his subordinates and little or none by him. To try to alter long-standing habits in one conference was impossible; Joe should have known it would take some time.

Of course, the attitude of employees toward their foreman directly affects their production. Joe should have known that too.

Case 8

John Doe has worked in Department Y for several years and has been a satisfactory employee in all respects. Recently he was appointed to a departmental safety committee and became deeply interested in safety work. He regards it as his responsibility to detect unsafe conditions, give safety tips to other men, and report any and all unsafe practices.

At first, this pleased John's foreman, and on several occasions the foreman commended John for his extra effort. Encouraged by this, John redoubled his vigilance. He began reading safety magazines, developed safety posters for his department, and offered his voluntary, spare-time service in the promotion of safety in his community.

Soon the foreman noticed that John's work was dropping off badly, apparently because he spent so much time away from his job on his safety activities. Since John was a tractor operator, his poor work on several occasions caused serious delay and much grumbling among the men he supplied. Also, John came to his foreman and reported that he had been threatened by some of the men to whom he had given "tips." On two occasions, the foreman had to intervene when other employees became angry at John for trying to tell them how to do their jobs more safely. It was charged that John was the foreman's spy, whose job it was to "get something on" the men.

Even though his safety efforts were of questionable value, John was encouraged by the plant safety director. The director felt that it was extremely important to encourage safety-consciousness and that it would seriously hinder his program if John were to be reprimanded. Such a reprimand might be considered an example of management's ingratitude for special safety effort. The safety director threatened to take up with top plant management any action the foreman might take to hinder John's safety work.

Situations are always difficult when a man is as dedicated to a good cause as John Doe seems to be. What happens now will depend considerably upon the degree to which management sincerely wants a good safety program.

John should not be reprimanded for neglecting his work because of his safety activities, nor should he be reprimanded for his tactless remarks to fellow workers. He should be taught that he is in a staff position as a member of the safety committee and that he must learn to use the noble art of persuasion. He should also be taught that his time and efforts in safety can only be expended as part of his regular work, not instead of it. The unsafe practices which he detects in the normal course of his work should be reported as such, not as violations by an individual. He should learn, finally, that his greatest weapon is the example he himself sets in following safe practices while doing his own work.

If the safety director should need a full-time assistant, John Doe might be considered a good candidate for transfer. He should not be transferred to another department to relieve the suspicion that he is his foreman's spy, nor should he be transferred to reduce his interest and activity in safety.

Case 9

Bill and Joe have worked together for about ten years in a maintenance department. They were good friends for a long time. Bill became a Mechanic A and Joe a Mechanic B on the same crew. Recently, however, they had some difficulties in their personal relationships outside the plant. Joe refused to endorse a note for Bill, and now the two are bitter enemies. They cooperate poorly on the job and have disrupted the morale of the entire crew. In addition, they have become known to the department and to other employees in the plant as troublemakers, poor workers, and hard fellows to get along with. It is recognized, nevertheless, until recently they were both topnotch men.

To relieve the situation, the foreman decided to have Bill change jobs with a Mechanic A from another crew. This move brought an immediate reaction from Bill's new crew. They came in a body to the foreman to protest the change. They felt that breaking up their "team" in that way would affect their production and reduce their earnings. After two weeks' trial, these assertions were borne out. Production was lower, and morale was becoming worse.

The foreman tried to find another job for Bill, but none was available at comparable work and pay levels. The foreman then returned Bill to his original crew, so that he was again working with

Joe, and thereby renewed the discontent of that crew. All the members, including Joe, are now obviously uncooperative with Bill.

Some people might suggest that if the foreman had just "let the matter ride," the difficulty would probably have disappeared in time. This could be a serious mistake; far from solving themselves, problems must be dealt with.

The major error in judgment here seems to be the foreman's transfer of Bill to another crew. Bill and the men of the new crew probably assumed that the foreman blamed Bill for the situation even though the foreman was in no position to place blame on anybody and, in any event, placing the blame never corrects a faulty situation.

Neither Bill or Joe should have been transferred. Both should have been called for an individual, personal confrontation with the foreman and talked to in terms of their substandard performance. The discussion in each case should have been based on facts and not on comparisons with others. Each man should have been given an opportunity to bring his performance back to standard within an agree-upon period of time. The foreman should have offered his help.

If, then, either or both men failed to get back to standard in the stipulated time, the foreman should have spoken to them again and probably extended the time for a short period. In this second confrontation, the foreman should have stated if they still did not "make the grade," they would be suspended without pay or discharged. Both confrontations should have been reported and filed; and, if Bill and Joe were union members, the union should receive copies.

Case 10

Bill is the operations general foreman on a battery of coke ovens. He is known as a production-minded foreman who is very severe with his men. For years he has kept his subordinates in a state of fear by strict and sometimes unfair disciplinary action. He has frequently subjected his men to unjust public criticism.

One morning, Bill came to work and found that his men had

"lost" three ovens on the morning turn. His turn foreman knew that this had been caused by negligence on the part of one of the men; but, in order to avoid unnecessary criticism for himself and excessive discipline for his men, the turn foreman reported that the old No. 3 pusher had broken down.

Bill immediately telephoned the electrical maintenance turn foreman, Sam, who was responsible for the pusher. Bill gave Sam a harsh verbal reprimand for the delay. Sam came to Bill's office; and, even though a group of Bill's men were present, he angrily announced that there had been no breakdown on the No. 3 pusher. Sam further stated that Bill was a blustering bully and that Bill had better get his own men to tell the truth before accusing others of making mistakes.

Bill reported Sam's conduct to his own superintendent and also to the maintenance superintendent with the recommendation that Sam be disciplined for insubordination and dishonesty.

In the first place, it is never good practice and, in fact, always bad practice for a foreman to falsify a report to his superior in order to protect his men.

Bill would have been well within the realm of good foremanship if he had accepted the statement of his turn foreman and turned to the maintenance department to find out the reasons for the breakdown and learn what preventive action might be taken for the future. If there was no evidence of a breakdown, Bill's problem then would be with his turn foreman. He should have determined from the turn foreman precisely what had caused the loss of the three ovens and ordered the necessary action.

Here is another case of passing the buck and fixing blame too hastily. This sort of thing often happens with a foreman who is so wholly production- or task-oriented that he is completely oblivious to the people involved. If the case had reached the general superintendent, Bill probably would have been severely reprimanded, warned, or possibly discharged.

INDEX

INDEX

D

Dickson, W. J., 17*n.*
Discipline, 75–87; decisions in enforcing, 84–87; making rules known, 77–80; need for rules, 75–77; rule enforcement, 80–83; and self-discipline, 83–84

E

Emerson, Harrington, 105
Employee application: checking of, 32; review of, 24–25
Employee selection, 21–35; interviewing, 25–32, 33; prior employers check, 32–33; recruiting, 22–24; reviewing the application, 24–25; testing, 34–35
Employee handbooks, 79

F

Fixtures, 115
Flow process chart, 110
Foreman: and department "climate," 16–17; duties and responsibilities of, 19–20; and first impressions, 37–38; as instructor, 14, 17–18; as manager, 14, 15, 16; and motivation, 58–61; and needs satisfaction, 58–61; as observer in employee selection, 33; origin of term, 13; as participant in employee selection, 33; potential role of in collective bargaining, 201–203; reluctance of to manage, 15–16; roles of, 14–15; as supervisor, 14, 15; and unions, 182–192
Foremanship, 14

G

Gantt, H. L., 105
Gilbreth, Frank B., 105
Goal setting, 62–64
Grievance machinery, in union contract, 197–199
Grievances: adjustment process, 96–99; areas of, 91–95; definition of, 89; development of, 89–91; types of, 95; warnings of, 95–96
Guild halls, 13

About the Author

FRANK A. BUSSE is the director of Administrative Services Division, Quality Bakers of America Cooperative, Inc.

A licensed professional engineer, Mr. Busse has been an adjunct professor of management at Newark College of Engineering Graduate School. He holds a B.S. in engineering from Newark College of Engineering and an LL.B.

Prior to his present position, Mr. Busse was an assistant professor at Newark College of Engineering, personnel manager of Falstrom Company, director of supervisory development for American Home Products Corporation, and director of personnel at Boyle-Midway Company (now an American Home Products subsidiary).

Mr. Busse is past president of the Northern New Jersey Chapter, Society for the Advancement of Management and a guest speaker and course leader for the American Management Association.